ANCIENT EGYPT

by Ippolito Rosellini

KU-305-712

CUMBRIA COUNTY LIBRARY	
H J	25/11/2003
932	£18.95

Contents

TEXT
Franco Serino

GRAPHIC DESIGN
Clara Zanotti

TRANSLATION
Richard Pierce

1
A PHARAOH MAKING OFFERINGS
THEBES, VALLEY OF THE KINGS
HISTORIC MONUMENTS, II
PLATE XVI,
DETAIL

A Ramesside ruler is offering incense burners to a divinity.

2-3
THE BATTLES AND VICTORIES OF RAMESSES II
ABU SIMBEL, GREAT TEMPLE
HISTORIC MONUMENTS, III
PLATE LXXXI

The pharaoh is depicted on a horse drawn chariot shooting an arrow at his enemies. His blue crown, a sort of military helmet, and his multicolored dress perfectly match the horses' ornaments, which are equally lavish. A vulture, the symbol of victory, hovers over the head of the sovereign.

4
SETI I WITH GODS
THEBES, TOMB OF SETI I
RELIGIOUS MONUMENTS
PLATE LIX

In this scene, painted by Nestor L'Hôte, the pharaoh has reached the Kingdom of the Dead and is accompanied by Horus, in the presence of Osiris, the most important god in the underworld.

5
OFFERINGS TO THE GODS
THEBES, TOMB OF RAMESSES III
RELIGIOUS MONUMENTS
PLATE LXXIV,
DETAIL

This woman carrying fruits typical of her homeland is taken from a parade of tribute-bearing individuals in the tomb of Ramesses III. Each of the figures in the scene symbolizes one of the forty-two provinces of Egypt during the Ramesside period. Hapi, the god of the Nile, completes the picture.

6-7
BATTLES AND VICTORIES OF RAMESSES II
ABU SIMBEL, GREAT TEMPLE
HISTORIC MONUMENTS, III
PLATE LXXXVI

This is the last of a series of plates depicting the triumphs of Ramesses II, who is in the act of presenting the Ethiopian and Nubian prisoners to the god Amun and the goddess Mut. The figure between the two divinities is Ramesses himself, who, in the guise of the sun god Ra, is protected by the goddess's embrace.

© 2003 White Star S.r.l.
Via C. Sassone, 22/24
13100 Vercelli, Italy
www.whitestar.it

ISBN 88-8095-903-4

Reprints:
1 2 3 4 5 6   07 06 05 04 03

Printed in Italy by Editoriale Johnson SpA
Seriate (BG), Italia
Color separation by Fotomec, Turin

All rights reserved. No part of this publication may be reproduced, stored in a retrieval system or transmitted in any form or by any means, electronic, mechanical, photocopying, recording or otherwise, without written permission from the publisher.

Ippolito Rosellini
AND THE REDISCOVERY OF
ANCIENT EGYPT IN THE NINETEENTH CENTURY

8
PORTRAIT OF ROSELLINI
PAINTING BY GIUSEPPE ANGELELLI

In this detail from the large painting of the *Franco-Tuscan Expedition to Egypt* (1828–29), executed by Giuseppe Angelelli, the Pisan Egyptologist, Ippolito Rosellini, is shown in Oriental dress and has a long beard.

Thanks to Napoleon's campaign in Egypt (1798-1801) and above all to the scientific expedition carried out at his behest, Europe rediscovered ancient Egyptian civilization two hundred years ago. The splendid engravings in Vivant Denon's *Voyage dans la Basse et la Haute Egypte* (1802) and the two editions of the *Description de l'Egypte* (1809 and 1821) were crucial to making known, as never before, the marvels of the land of the Nile.

While all credit is due to France and the eminent scientist Jean-François Champollion for having revealed the final secret in deciphering ancient Egyptian hieroglyphs twenty years later, Italy deserves her share of glory as the birthplace of an illustrious citizen who became the pupil and spiritual heir of Champollion—Ippolito Rosellini, 'the father of Italian Egyptology.'

Ippolito Rosellini was born in Pisa on August 13, 1800, and soon revealed an aptitude for 'cultivating letters.' In fact, at the tender age of seventeen he was already devoting his energies to the study of Hebrew and the history of the Catholic Church at the local university. He earned his degree in theology in 1821 and moved to Bologna to follow the courses in Oriental languages under the famous polyglot and Orientalist, Giuseppe Mezzofanti. After returning to Pisa, Rosellini, who had just turned twenty-four, was appointed lecturer of Oriental languages and Hebrew at the University of Pisa.

When he found out about the decipherment of Egyptian hieroglyphs, illustrated by Champollion in his famous *Précis du système hiéroglyphique* which was published in 1824, he immediately devoted himself with passion to the study of this new discipline, partly in order not to remain "within the regrettable limits of mediocrity."

H. Rosellini

In the summer of 1825, almost certainly in Florence, he met the "Decipherer" (as Rosellini was fond of calling the great French scholar), who had gone to Italy the preceding year to study the Drovetti Collection at Turin and other collections of ancient Egyptian objects. "Because of that secret law of nature," he recalled, "that binds those souls who are molded in unison and carry out the same studies, we had hardly seen each other that we were already friends. I was no sooner taken into his friendship and generously informed about his secrets and discoveries, than I felt grow more sharply and deeply in my heart a love for Egypt; and I immediately determined to follow him wherever he should go."

Apropos of the decipherment of Egyptian writing, at the end of that year, the young Pisan published a paper in which he set forth (" . . . at the level of even the less educated readers") Champollion's discovery and defended the latter from his detractors, such as Lanci, Cordero di San Quintino, and Seyffarth. This work was much appreciated by the French Egyptologist for its clarity and conciseness.

In the spring of the following year Rosellini saw Champollion again, as he had returned to Italy to study more ancient Egyptian artifacts, visit other Italian cities and take possession of British Consul Henry Salt's collection, which he had already examined and which had just been purchased by the French government.

The two scholars spent four months together, which cemented their deep and sincere friendship even more. Rosellini was to become the "Decipherer's" (as Champollion was sometimes known) favorite disciple and the latter even went so far as to call him "… mon fidèle compagnon et élève… jeune homme plein d'esprit' ('my faithful companion and pupil, a young man full of spirit'). And Champollion wrote to his brother: "I have noted (in the researches I made in Rome and Naples) the young professor's true passion for serious studies, his total devotion to science, while at the same time appreciating the winning qualities that so distinguish him. Egyptian archaeology has made a profitable acquisition with him . . . . I myself would be happy, in associating with him in my studies on Egypt, to furnish him with the means to progress in the other branches of philology he is cultivating with such enthusiasm and commitment . . . . The subject is so vast that at times I feel both the impossibility of succeeding all by myself and the need of a collaborator so devoted to science as Rosellini."

Further demonstration of Champollion's esteem for the young Pisan scholar was his request, made a few months later, to Leopold II of Tuscany, an illuminated as well as ambitious ruler, to allow Rosellini to finish his specialist studies of Oriental languages and hieroglyphs at Paris.

After being granted permission to leave (and to take a year's leave from his teaching duties), Rosellini set off for the French capital in December 1826. He stopped off at Turin on the way to meet the Orientalist Amedeo Peyron and friar Costanzo Gazzera, a lecturer in philosophy and passionate linguist. This marked the beginning of a long friendship between Gazzera and the Pisan scholar that is attested by their long correspondence, which went on from 1826 to 1840.

During his sojourn in Paris, which lasted seven months, Rosellini helped his "dear Maestro" to classify and put in order the Salt Collection and Drovetti's second collection, which had recently been purchased by the Louvre Museum.

9 top
THE COURSE OF THE SUN
IN THE AFTERLIFE
THEBES, TOMB OF TAUSERT/SETHNAKHTE
RELIGIOUS MONUMENTS
PLATE LXX, DETAIL

A symbolic scene concerning the birth of a new day, or dawn.

9 bottom
THE HAWK-HEADED GOD
RA-HORAKHTY
THEBES, TOMB OF MERENEPTAH
HISTORIC MONUMENTS, III
PLATE CXVIII, DETAIL

The god Ra-Horakhty with the symbol of eternal life (ankh) in his left hand.

JEAN-FRANÇOIS CHAMPOLLION
PORTRAIT BY LÉON COGNIET

A passionate student of ancient Oriental languages at an early age, Champollion took the first step in the decipherment of hieroglyphic script in 1808, when he began to study a copy of the Rosetta Stone, which Captain Bouchard had found in 1799 and is now kept in the British Museum. After years of constant devotion to his studies, thanks to his intuition and knowledge of languages, the French scholar was finally able to announce he had succeeded in interpreting ancient Egyptian script in September 1822.

He studied with unswerving passion, met some French Orientalists, and had many talks with Champollion concerning the plans for a Franco-Tuscan expedition in Egypt, whose aim was to make a scientific exploration of the ruins of that ancient civilization and gain definitive confirmation of the discovery and decipherment of hieroglyphs.

When he returned to Italy in July 1827, Rosellini presented the project to Grand Duke Leopold II, who approved it with great interest and guaranteed the necessary financing. In September, Rosellini went back to Paris to find out whether the plan had been approved by the French government, which had seemed rather averse to the scientific mission. The following month, the Pisan scholar put his sentiments before his love of Egypt and married Zenobia, the daughter of the famous composer Luigi Cherubini whom he had met the preceding year. She bore him four children, including a girl who died while still quite young.

In the early months of 1828, the last obstacles to the mission were overcome; it was finally approved and financed by King Charles X as well. The mission began its work in July of that year and ended in the autumn of 1829. The most important events in the journey to Egypt and Nubia–including comments on the research, on the discovery of various archaeological sites, and on the joint work–were noted down in the interesting travel journal written by Rosellini and published by Gabrieli in 1925.

When he returned to Pisa in January 1830, Rosellini devoted his energy to rearranging the vast scientific material he had prepared in Egypt. In July 1831 he went back to Paris to plan the publication of a work with Champollion. However, the premature death of his mentor in March 1832, plus a sort of unjustified mistrust of Rosellini on the part of Champollion's brother, known as Champollion-Figeac, prevented the results of the mission from being published together, so that two large works came out separately.

In 1834 and 1835, Rosellini–due to his outstanding merit, and for the first time in Italy–held courses in the Coptic and ancient Egyptian languages at the University of Pisa and was appointed university librarian by Grand Duke Leopold II.

Rosellini had by then become a leading figure in Egyptology, receiving recognition and testimonials from various international academies and representatives of European culture.

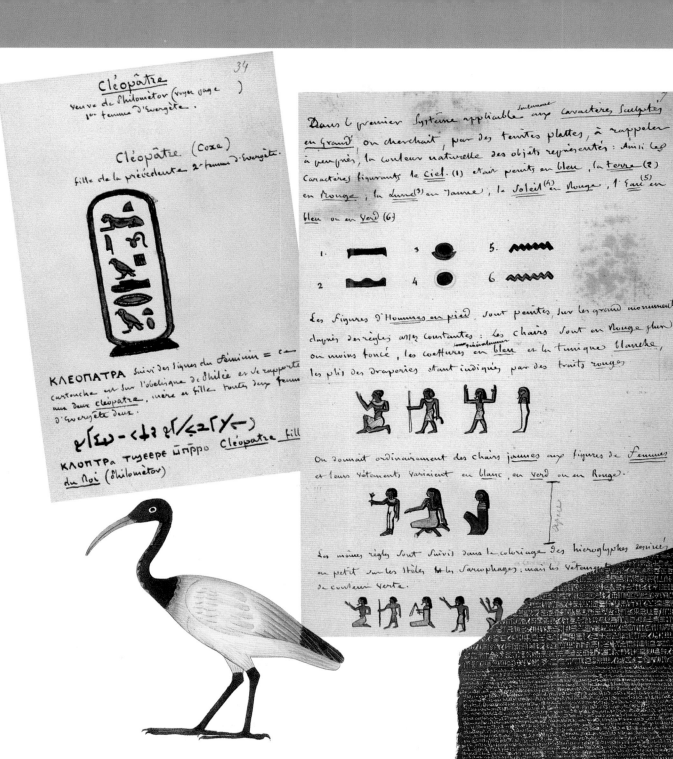

For example, in 1836 the young German scholar Richard Lepsius went to Pisa to finish his studies under Rosellini's guidance, and two years later the Dutchman Conrad Leemans, then director of the Leiden Museum, began a long and fruitful correspondence with him. Rosellini initiated an equally interesting exchange of letters, which lasted for years, with leading Italian men of letters, archaeologists such as Luigi Maria Ungarelli, and the already mentioned Gazzera and Peyron.

From 1838 to 1841, Rosellini's often frenetic efforts to finish his various work commitments and the increasingly bitter polemics that continued for years all contributed to weakening his health, which was already precarious because of lung and intestinal illnesses. Like his dear "Maestro," he also died prematurely, in Pisa, on June 4, 1843.

11 TOP
LA GRAMMAIRE EGYPTIENNE

In his *Grammaire Egyptienne*, two manuscript pages of which are reproduced here, Champollion reaffirmed his conviction that hieroglyphic script was at the same time figurative, symbolic, and phonetic.

11 BOTTOM RIGHT
THE ROSETTA STONE

Champollion compared Ptolemy's cartouche, which appears several times in this famous stela, with Cleopatra's, which was carved on an obelisk found at Philae, and this provided him with the virtually definitive confirmation of his method of decipherment.

The Franco-Tuscan Expedition in Egypt

1828-29

12-13
THE FRANCO-TUSCAN
EXPEDITION
PAINTING BY GIUSEPPE ANGELELLI

This canvas (3.47 x 2.28 m) executed by Giuseppe Angelelli ca. 1835, portrays all the members of the Franco-Tuscan expedition. The artist set the scene among the ruins of ancient Thebes, but the natural scenery in the background is for the most part imaginary. The persons portrayed–almost all of whom are in Oriental dress–are, from left to right: the French illustrator Albert Bertin (barely visible), Salvador Cherubini, Alessandro Ricci (in a red tunic), Nestor L'Hôte, and a richly attired dragoman, or interpreter. Behind L'Hôte is Angelelli, who is holding a piece of paper. Next to him are Pierre Lehoux, Giuseppe Raddi (seated, looking at some plants in his lap), and two Egyptians. In the foreground, almost lying on the ground, is the French painter Alexandre Duchesne. Standing in the middle of the painting are Rosellini, who is holding a drawing in his left hand, and behind him, his uncle Gaetano. Champollion is seated on a rock, with a thick beard, and is holding a saber that Mohammed Ali gave him; at his feet are some objects the group just found.
The bare-chested man is the foreman of the excavation laborers.
The last figure is the local sheikh, who is indicating other sites to be discovered.

Some of the seventeen articles of the
regulation that the Franco-Tuscan
Expedition observed during its research.

The close friendship between Rosellini and
Champollion gave birth to the idea of a
common mission in the land of the pharaohs.
Despite King Charles X's irresolution in this regard,
the grand duke of Tuscany, Leopold II, as we have
already seen, was enthusiastic about the project and
promoted the first international scientific mission
that aimed at the "exploration of the surviving
historic monuments in Egypt."

Compared to Napoleon's expedition, this one
set out not only to illustrate and describe most of
the remains of ancient Egypt that could still be
seen, but thanks to the newly gained ability to
interpret hieroglyphic writing, also to make a
targeted and systematic study of the antiquities in
this recently rediscovered country.

There were fourteen members of this mission.

The French team consisted of:
• Jean-François Champollion;
• Antoine Bibent, a young architect who soon had to
leave his colleagues and return to France due to illness;
• Nestor L'Hôte;
• Alexandre Duchesne;
• Albert Henry Bertin and
• Pierre François Lehoux, all of whom were
illustrators.

The Tuscan team was made up of the following
persons:
• Ippolito Rosellini;
• Gaetano Rosellini, Ippolito's uncle, an architect and
engineer;
• Alessandro Ricci, a physician and illustrator;
• Giuseppe Angelelli, a painter and illustrator;
• Giuseppe Raddi, a naturalist;
• Gaetano Galastri, Raddi's assistant, who soon had to
return to Italy because of a foot injury;
• Salvador Cherubini, an illustrator and Rosellini's
brother-in-law, a naturalized Italian. Although he
was officially part of the Tuscan team, he was at the
disposal of both.

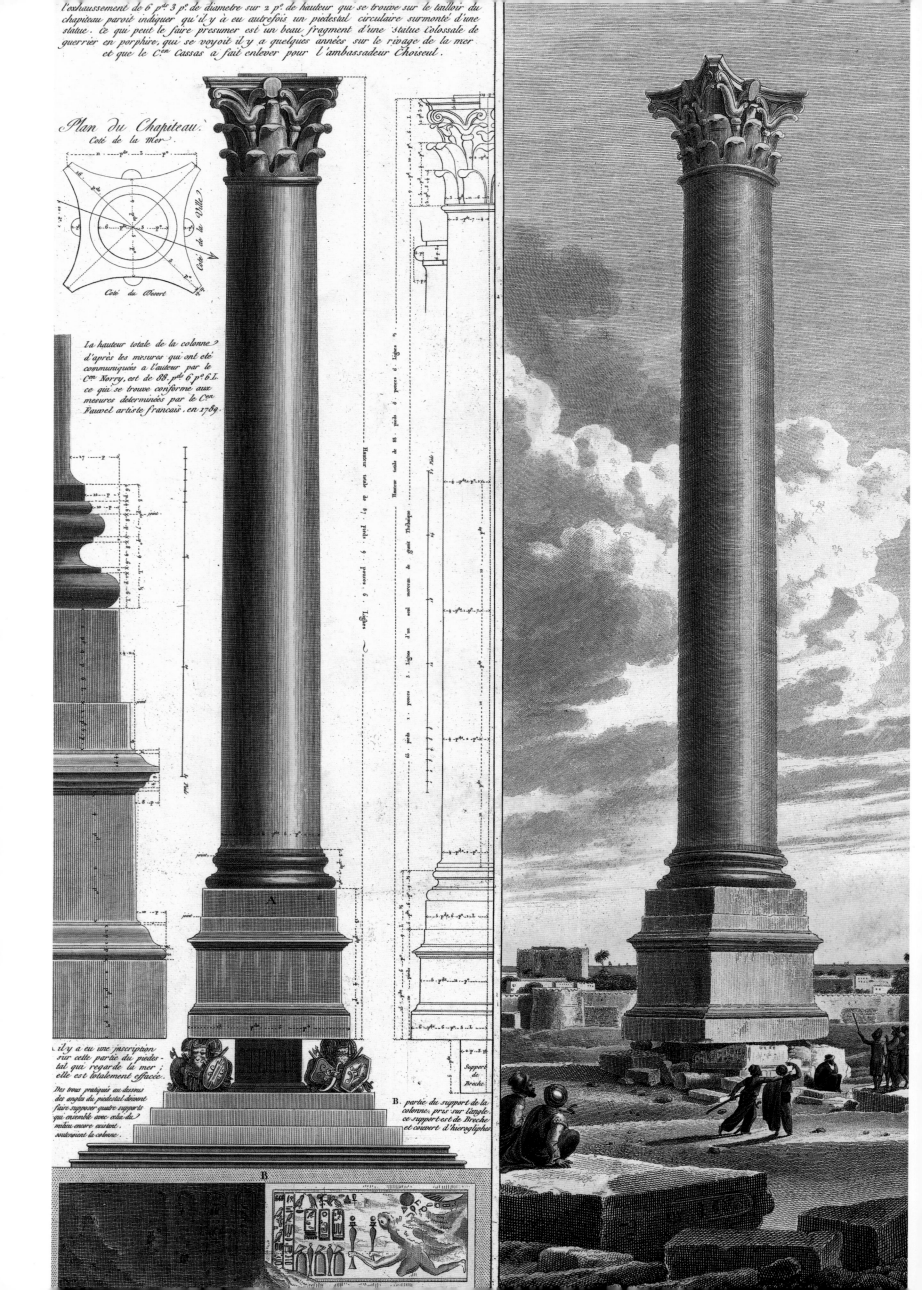

l'exhaussement de 6 p.ds 3 p. de diametre sur 2 p. de hauteur qui se trouve sur le tailloir du chapiteau paroit indiquer qu'il y à eu autrefois un piedestal circulaire surmonté d'une statue. Ce qui peut le faire presumer est un beau fragment d'une statue Colossale de guerrier en porphire, qui se voyoit il y a quelques années sur le rivage de la mer et que le C.en Cassas a fait enlever pour l'ambassadeur Choiseul.

Plan du Chapiteau.
Coté de la Mer.

Coté de la Ville?

Coté du Desert

La hauteur totale de la colonne d'après les mesures qui ont été communiquées a l'auteur par le C.en Norry, est de 88.pds 6 p. 6 l. ce qui se trouve conforme aux mesures determinées par le C.en Fauvel artiste francais, en 1789.

A

il y a eu une inscription sur cette partie du piedestal qui regarde la mer, elle est totalement effacée.

Des trous pratiqués au dessus des angles du piedestal doivent faire supposer quatre supports qui ensemble avec celui du milieu encore existant soutenoient la colonne.

B. partie du support de la colonne, pris sur l'angle, ce support est de Breche et couvert d'hieroglyphes

Support de Breche

B

The Journey to Egypt and Nubia

The French corvette *Eglé* set sail from Toulon on July 31, 1828, with the fourteen original members of the mission, and after a brief stop in Sicily, arrived in Alexandria on August 18.

The first leg of the journey to Egypt, which Champollion and Rosellini in particular had set their heart on, had been reached. The first few days after landing were given over to meeting with the local authorities and European diplomats, including Carlo Rossetti, the consul general of Tuscany, and Bernardino Drovetti, who for years had been the consular delegate of France.

The stay in the city founded by Alexander the Great in 331 BC lasted for about a month, during which time the group visited the most important quarters and became acquainted with the traditions and customs of the Egyptians. The most famous monuments, which could be seen even then, were a pair of obelisks known as 'Cleopatra's Needles,' and a column called 'Pompey's Pillar.' Apropos of the first two monoliths (one of which had fallen in the fourteenth century), we know that they had been transported from Heliopolis during the Augustan age, when the city, a metropolis with 300,000 inhabitants, was the 'emporium of the world' and a brilliant cultural center. Nothing is known about when the curious name of the last queen of Egypt was given to the obelisks. Both of them left Egypt in the mid-1800s. The one that had fallen was donated to Great Britain and is now in London: it was placed along the Thames in 1878; the other, donated to the United States, was set up in Central Park in New York City in 1881.

While examining the obelisk that was still standing, Rosellini noted "excavations around the base . . . were carried out in such an irregular manner that one is led to believe attempts were made to knock it down." The name given to 'Pompey's Pillar' has no historical basis. It was connected to the memory of the death of Pompey, who was killed in 48 BC along the Egyptian coast, to which he had fled after being defeated by Caesar. In reality the column, which is over twenty-one meters high and has a Corinthian capital, was erected in the late third century AD in honor of Emperor Diocletian.

14 AND 15
POMPEY'S PILLAR
AND CLEOPATRA'S NEEDLES
LITHOGRAPHS BY LOUIS-FRANÇOIS CASSAS

These lithographs of two monuments in Alexandria–'Pompey's Pillar,' at left, and one of 'Cleopatra's Needles,' at right–were made by the French artist Louis-François Cassas (1756–1827), who visited Egypt in 1785 during a journey to the Near East. Both engravings were taken from his *Voyage Pittorique de la Syrie, de la Phoenicie, de la Palestine et de la Basse Egypte,* which included 180 plates and was published in Paris in 1799.

Egypt at the Time of the Franco-Tuscan Expedition

At the dawn of the nineteenth century, Egypt was a huge province of the Ottoman Empire that for some time had been weakened by internal strife and a very weak economy, and seemed to be stagnating in a sort of medieval limbo. With Napoleon's expedition the country came into contact with new institutions that triggered hope for renewal and the rise of a new era. And, in fact, a political and social turning point came about with the man considered the founder of modern Egypt, Mohammed Ali.

Bold and courageous as well as unscrupulous and cruel, this leader initiated a vast reform program in all fields. Well aware of the importance of Western civilization, Mohammed Ali

did not hesitate to make use of European experts and advisers. As a result, in the early decades of the nineteenth century, travelers, technicians, explorers, and adventurers poured into the country in search of antiquities. As far as the field of archaeology is concerned, several foreign diplomats devoted all their energy to the search for finds to be set on display in the museums and collections of their respective countries. This sort of antiquities hunt was not always characterized by fair play, to say the least; in fact, it was sometimes accompanied by gunshots.

On September 14, after managing to get the necessary *firmans*, or decrees, authorizing them to travel and carry out digs and research in the different localities of Egypt, the members of the mission set off for Cairo in two boats. Because of a painful sore on his foot, the young Galastri could not continue the journey and was forced to return to Italy.

They navigated for one week among villages and thick vegetation. "The shores of the Nile," Rosellini wrote, "continue to delight one because of the crops and luxuriant greenery that covers them. Cotton, hemp, and other plants grow most beautifully . . . . Tamarisk and Nilotic mimosa are quite abundant." And again: "The Nile persists in being charming and green on both banks, which have many villages. The people are distrustful and afraid of us at first . . . but they soon realize our intentions and all the children gather around us to watch us with curiosity, or with the hope of getting a para [coin]."

On September 20, the mission members disembarked at Boulaq, at that time a river port of Cairo, and went to the nearby metropolis, which, in that season, was quite lively because of the important feast in honor of the birth of the Prophet. "The overall view of Cairo has nothing in common with our life," we read in Rosellini. He continues: "The broad expanse of the square was filled with people: voices crying out, bagpipes and fifes playing . . . the cry of acrobats who entertain large circles of people with their clever tricks and with the dances of the *cynocephali*, a large and lovely species of baboon, which was a sacred animal in ancient Egypt. The constant to and fro of small donkeys, camels, dromedaries, and horses that knock their way through the crowd, amid the shouts of the muleteers, riders, and the people; the clothes, voices, words—in short, everything is new, bizarre, and indescribable."

The time spent at Cairo was used to observe other ceremonies and visit the various parts of the city, with its characteristic bazaars, mosques, and the tombs of the caliphs, which at the time were fine examples of Islamic architecture.

Rosellini's note regarding the vile slave market, which continued to thrive in Egypt until the mid-nineteenth century, is quite moving: "In one of those large square houses," he observes, "are the male and female slaves that are sold in Cairo. There is a great number of them and the sight is at once pitiful and interesting . . . ."

16
THE FOUNTAIN OF TUSUN PASHA
ENGRAVING BY ROBERT HAY

The fountain of Tusun Pasha, dating from the early nineteenth century, in an engraving reproduced from Robert Hay's *Illustrations of Cairo* (1840).

17
FOUNTAIN OF NAFISA
ENGRAVING BY ROBERT HAY

This fountain is a typical example of Islamic art and architecture. The illustration is again by Robert Hay, the British traveler and illustrator (1799-1869) who visited Egypt several times between 1818 and 1838. Among his assistants, Owen Browne Carter and Charles Laver are particularly worthy of mention.

18 TOP LEFT
QUEEN ISIS
HISTORIC MONUMENTS, I
PLATE VIII, DETAIL

This drawing shows Queen Isis,
Ramesses VI's mother, whose tomb lies
in the Valley of the Queens.

18 BOTTOM RIGHT
BIRDS AMONG PAPYRUS PLANTS
BENI HASAN
CIVIL MONUMENTS, I
PLATE XIV, DETAIL

This is a drawing of a nest of ibises
among papyrus plants.

18-19
VIEW OF THE NECROPOLIS
OF BENI HASAN
CIVIL MONUMENTS, I
PLATE I, DETAIL

This drawing is a view of the important
Middle Kingdom (2000–1800 BC)
archaeological site about 299
kilometers south of Cairo.

19
EXAMPLE
OF A LOTUS STEM COLUMN
BENI HASAN
CIVIL MONUMENTS, II
PLATE XIV, DETAIL

This column, a typical element in the
architecture of the Beni Hasan tombs,
is a stylized representation of a bunch
of lotus flowers tied together.
This sort of flared corolla was the
capital of the column.

After a few days spent in Memphis, which bore hardly any traces of its former grandeur and which a dismayed Rosellini described as "now in a heap of scraps," the mission camped in nearby Saqqara to visit the site so rich in Old Kingdom tombs and pyramids, copy the sculptures and paintings, and carry out digs with the aid of young locals.

After passing through illness and indisposition caused by the fatigue and conditions of life (which were often quite difficult by European standards), the mission rode on camels and donkeys to Giza, the plateau with the pyramids and the Sphinx, which at that time was half buried in the sand.

These famous monuments, described and drawn by hundreds of travelers, impressed the mission members, who did not hesitate to go up to the top of the Pyramid of Khufu (or Cheops), from where they could admire the plain where the famous battle between Napoleon and the Mamluks had taken place thirty years earlier.

With these recollections, which were rounded off by their first archaeological experience and with interesting drawings executed, on October 11, 1828, the group resumed navigation southward and on October 22 reached a locality in Middle Egypt known as Beni Hasan. When they landed, the travelers began

to inspect the surrounding area, which was delimited by hills or average-sized mountains. "The Arab mountain, cut vertically," the *Journal* says, "for a long stretch consists of rock-hewn caves, which we climbed up to visit and found more beautiful than any others we had seen till then."

Instead of staying one day as planned, the expedition remained there two weeks. In fact, there were many extremely interesting tombs of local governors, such as those of Amenemhet and Khnumhotep. For the most part cut out of the limestone rock, and aligned with a type of column that Champollion called "Proto-Doric," the tombs enraptured all the members of the group, who worked ceaselessly to copy the wall paintings, "true tempera paintings, remarkable for the delicacy and beauty of their draughtmanship" (Champollion).

The many scenes of domestic and civic life, which were reproduced in four hundred drawings, were the most beautiful the scholars had seen so far in Egypt: agriculture, livestock breeding, arts and crafts, games, music, dance–all flowed before their eyes, together with a series of figures and animals made vivid by colors which were still fresh and lovely in the early nineteenth century, but which now have been either ruined or have disappeared.

After their visit to Beni Hasan and other nearby localities, the expedition ventured a few miles further to see Antinoopolis, once the lovely city of the emperor Hadrian, and Hermopolis, which is another important archaeological site. According to Rosellini, both places, however, were reduced to rubble, "because of the devastating barbarism of the government and inhabitants."

They landed a little farther southward and found "an unknown city" which interested them but could not be identified: it was Tell al-Amarna, the city of Akhenaten, the 'heretic' pharaoh.

As was only natural, during the journey, some days were busier than others. They would land to buy supplies, visit villages or take part in dinners or parties organized by the *kashef*s (district inspectors) during which smoking the typical narghile pipes and watching dances by the local beauties were part of the routine.

20-21 TOP
GYMNASTIC-MILITARY SCENES
TOMBS AT BENI HASAN AND ASYUT
CIVIL MONUMENTS, III
PLATE CXVII, DETAIL

Soldiers armed with clubs, bows, arrows, and shields drilling in attack and defense.

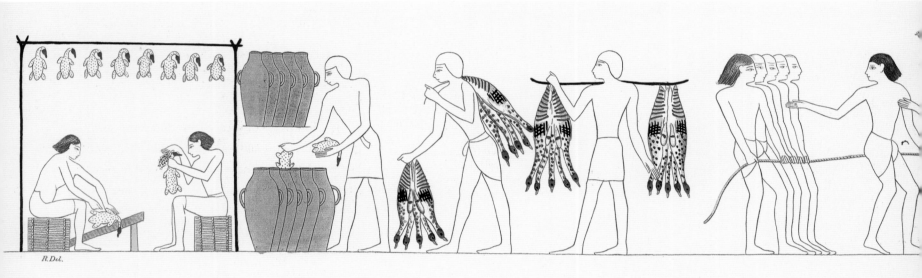

On November 16, after visiting villages or towns on either side of the Nile, such as Asyut and Akhmim, the expedition arrived at Dendera, a place the French and Italian travelers had often heard about. They made their first excursion to see the ruins of the ancient city at night. After walking a few miles, the group came within sight of a large temple which, on the left-hand bank of the Nile, was illuminated by moonlight. "The appearance of the sky, the silence of the night, and the presence of these plants, so varied and beautiful (dum palms, sycamores, and so on), made for a wholly singular scene"–this was the first impression noted down by Rosellini in his travel journal. "Further on we caught sight of the large gate that afforded access to the vast precinct of the great temple . . . . We were struck with deep admiration for such an elegant structure and such harmonious lines . . . . 'How lovely it is!' we all said in unison.

20-21 BOTTOM
A JOURNEY DOWN THE NILE
TOMB IN BENI HASAN
CIVIL MONUMENTS, III
PLATE CIX, DETAIL

20-21 CENTER
DUCK HUNT
THEBAN TOMB
CIVIL MONUMENTS, I
PLATE IV, DETAIL

The scene shows a large hexagonal net stretched out in a lake and secured with a pole and rope. A man, hidden among the plants, is signaling when the rope should be pulled to catch the birds. The captured birds (left) are taken to a hut where they are killed, plucked, salted, and placed in large jars.

An illustration of a boat with twelve rowers who are busy mooring. Inside the cabin are the women of the harem.

And we set out to the temple near at hand that loomed so immensely in front of us . . . . Such was our surprise, amazement, astonishment, that we were speechless at that moment. The night and the lights made an impression that human language could not describe."

The following day was lovely and sunny and the group returned to admire the temple of the goddess Hathor. The monument was begun under the last Ptolemaic rulers in the first century BC and was finished in the Roman period, so it is one of the last artistic manifestations of ancient Egyptian civilization.

A favorable wind made the short trip to legendary Thebes even easier. The group arrived there on November 20, remaining only one week for an initial reconnaissance of the ruins of the ancient site, which now includes the famous localities of Luxor and Karnak. The good weather conditions of this season made it imperative to go to Nubia first; they would make a much longer stay at Thebes on their return trip.

The mission resumed its journey, visiting other interesting archaeological sites such as ancient Hermonthis, with the ruins of a temple, and then Esna, called Latopolis by the Greeks. After visiting the large Roman-period temple, which was still mostly buried in the sand, the group decided to make an excursion to the ruins of a locality called Contra-Lato on the left-hand bank of the Nile just opposite Esna. "The French Commission," Rosellini wrote, "had already drawn the small temple with Contra-Lato [a city given this name because it lay opposite Latopolis], and we went to see it."

After following several rough paths, ferrying on a boat, and a long walk through the fields, almost all the members of the mission reached the indicated spot, but they did not see anything. "We made inquiries of an old Arab who protected the *durra* [a variety of sorghum] from the birds," Rosellini wrote in his *Journal*, "and, pointing to a pile of whitish scraps, he told us that it had been destroyed a few days earlier at the behest of the *nádir* [local governor]. Our indignation and anger were all the stronger because we could not know or understand the reason for this. Now we already knew that the Turkish leaders often destroyed ancient monuments made of limestone in order to make lime mortar, but the temple at Contra-Lato was made of sandstone, which could not serve this purpose . . . . Therefore, only because of age-old barbarism, ever more ruthless and resurgent, was this temple destroyed."

With Rosellini's bitter comment in mind, let us continue the description of the journey. At the end of November, the mission reached Edfu, a village known for the temple dedicated to the god Horus. After seeing the monument, begun in 327 BC under Ptolemy III and completed in the first decades of the Christian era, the Pisan scholar noted that it was "one of best preserved in all Egypt . . . ," but most of it was buried in the sand. Furthermore, "the Arabs have encumbered all this large edifice by building their miserable Nilotic mud huts inside and outside it."

Still going up the Nile, the mission stopped off at Gebel al-Silsila to visit the sandstone quarries and then at Kom Ombo, a place known for another Ptolemaic-age temple. On December 4, 1828, it arrived at Aswan, an important locality in Nubia, the gateway to black Africa.

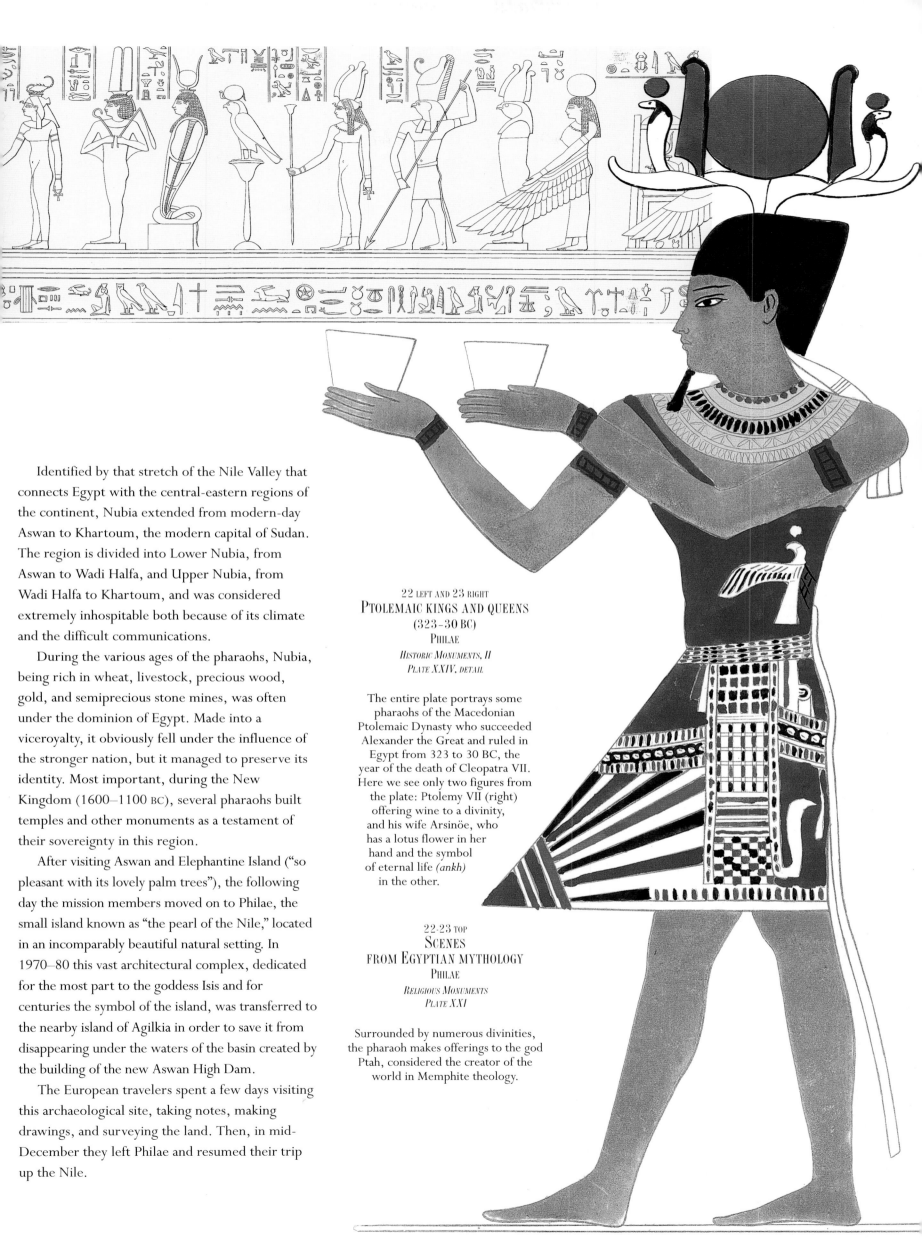

Identified by that stretch of the Nile Valley that connects Egypt with the central-eastern regions of the continent, Nubia extended from modern-day Aswan to Khartoum, the modern capital of Sudan. The region is divided into Lower Nubia, from Aswan to Wadi Halfa, and Upper Nubia, from Wadi Halfa to Khartoum, and was considered extremely inhospitable both because of its climate and the difficult communications.

During the various ages of the pharaohs, Nubia, being rich in wheat, livestock, precious wood, gold, and semiprecious stone mines, was often under the dominion of Egypt. Made into a viceroyalty, it obviously fell under the influence of the stronger nation, but it managed to preserve its identity. Most important, during the New Kingdom (1600–1100 BC), several pharaohs built temples and other monuments as a testament of their sovereignty in this region.

After visiting Aswan and Elephantine Island ("so pleasant with its lovely palm trees"), the following day the mission members moved on to Philae, the small island known as "the pearl of the Nile," located in an incomparably beautiful natural setting. In 1970–80 this vast architectural complex, dedicated for the most part to the goddess Isis and for centuries the symbol of the island, was transferred to the nearby island of Agilkia in order to save it from disappearing under the waters of the basin created by the building of the new Aswan High Dam.

The European travelers spent a few days visiting this archaeological site, taking notes, making drawings, and surveying the land. Then, in mid-December they left Philae and resumed their trip up the Nile.

22 LEFT AND 23 RIGHT
PTOLEMAIC KINGS AND QUEENS
(323–30 BC)
PHILAE
HISTORIC MONUMENTS, II
PLATE XXIV, DETAIL

The entire plate portrays some pharaohs of the Macedonian Ptolemaic Dynasty who succeeded Alexander the Great and ruled in Egypt from 323 to 30 BC, the year of the death of Cleopatra VII. Here we see only two figures from the plate: Ptolemy VII (right) offering wine to a divinity, and his wife Arsinöe, who has a lotus flower in her hand and the symbol of eternal life *(ankh)* in the other.

22-23 TOP
SCENES
FROM EGYPTIAN MYTHOLOGY
PHILAE
RELIGIOUS MONUMENTS
PLATE XXI

Surrounded by numerous divinities, the pharaoh makes offerings to the god Ptah, considered the creator of the world in Memphite theology.

HOMAGE TO AMUN
RELIGIOUS MONUMENTS
PLATE XLI, detail

Presented by Ra-Horakhty, Amenophis III kneels before the god Amun, who is seated in his naos (shrine).

Since Napoleon's Commission had not gone beyond this locality, little was known of the region. However, it must be said that in January 1738 the Danish explorer Frederik Ludwig Norden (1708-42) went as far as al-Derr, a locality that no other European had ever reached since the time of the 'Anonymous Venetian' (1589). In any case, Norden was the first person to draw and describe–albeit with some errors–most of the temples in Lower Nubia. And in 1812-14, with luck and courage, the British traveler Thomas Legh (1793-1857) managed to reach Qasr Ibrim, fifty kilometers north of Abu Simbel.

The mission continued its trip, making many stops to visit the numerous temples that stood along the banks of the Nile for about 300 kilometers, from Dabod to Qertassi, from Dendur to al-Dakka and on, up to al-Derr and Qasr Ibrim (from 1960 to 1980, under the auspices of the UNESCO Nubian Rescue Campaign, all these temples were dismantled, cut into blocks and then transferred to higher places).

On December 26 they reached Abu Simbel, which has become world famous because of the two temples built by Ramesses II around 1250 BC. As regards the larger temple, its existence was unknown until 1813

because it had been built in an isolated area and for centuries was totally covered by the sand. On March 22 of that year, the legendary Swiss explorer and Orientalist Johann Ludwig Burckhardt (1784-1817), who had already found Petra in 1812, achieved his second archaeological exploit by revealing the existence of the Great Temple of Abu Simbel to the world.

The Franco-Tuscan mission first visited the smaller temple dedicated to Queen Nefertari, then went to the larger one, the "abode of millions of years," built to exalt the power and divinity of Ramesses II. Champollion had the following to say about the Abu Simbel temple: "It alone is worth the journey to Nubia: it is a wonder that would be exceptional even in Thebes."

Rosellini's comment was almost identical: "This edifice hewn entirely in equal measure out of the rock is the most astonishing in all of Nubia. The façade is decorated with four enormous seated colossi . . . the sands cover the entrance and the colossi above the knees . . . . Over sixty men tried to make a hole in order to penetrate inside and their fatigue was almost in vain because of the huge quantity of sand that fell

THE MYTH OF OSIRIS
PHILAE
RELIGIOUS MONUMENTS
PLATE XVI, detail

Plate XVI contains scenes that decorated the walls of the Temple of Isis on the island of Philae. This detail shows the mummy of Osiris lying on a crocodile and aided by Isis, Harpocrates (Horus the Child), and Atum. According to legend, one of the many tombs of the god of the dead lay on the island of Philae.

back as soon as they removed it . . . . Finally, towards evening they made a small opening . . . . Some of our men who went into the first entrance found the temperature much like that of a stoke-hole."

The following day the two mission leaders and Ricci made the first visit to the interior, which was made even more difficult by the high temperature. However, dripping with sweat "much more than when entering a Turkish bath," they went in and observed "… the main hall of the temple, which is vast and supported by two rows of four large pillars each, upon which rest, like caryatids, eight colossi at least thirty ells high. The walls are all covered with painted historic low reliefs."

After deciding to stay for a longer period on their return trip, on December 30 the mission members went to the last destination of their journey, Wadi Halfa, the locality where the Second Cataract once stood (it is now underwater in the artificial Nasser basin). Only one day was given over to visiting the area, exploring among the ruins of temples, limestone rocks, and verdant islets in the middle of the large river. After the first five months of their journey, at Wadi Halfa, "after firing a shot with the cannon and letting out a universal cry of joy, we began to descend the Nile . . . ." This was on January 1, 1829.

The second stay at Abu Simbel lasted from January 3 to 16. During this time all the members of the mission resumed their work—in shifts of no more than three or four hours due to the torrid heat—copying and drawing the splendid reliefs; especially those in the Great Temple, where the sand had been removed from the entrance. The mission continued its descent of the Nile, making stops to see (or see again) other Nubian temples such as those at Wadi al-Sebua, al-Maharraq, Tafa, and Kalabsha.

25 LEFT
SETI I'S VICTORIES
KARNAK, TEMPLE OF AMUN
HISTORIC MONUMENTS, III
PLATE LX

This iconographic motif, often seen on the pylons or walls of Egyptian temples, shows the pharaoh defeating his enemies. Under his feet are the foreign nations subject to his rule.

25 RIGHT
A PRISONER
BEIT AL-WALI, NUBIA
HISTORIC MONUMENTS, III
PLATE LXIII

The image of Seti I holding an Asian prisoner held by the hair is from the small Nubian rock-cut temple at Beit al-Wali.

26 LEFT
THE OBELISK AT LUXOR
THEBES, TEMPLE OF AMUN-RA
HISTORIC MONUMENTS, III
PLATE CXVII, DETAIL

This is a detail of one of the
obelisks that Ramesses II had built
in front of the pylon of the temple
at Luxor. The entire plate includes
all sides of the two obelisks, one
of which has stood in the Place
de la Concorde in Paris since 1836.

On February 1, the group arrived at Philae and
was at Aswan a week later. After a visit at the granite
quarries, navigation resumed (with a few hours of
rain), heading for already explored sites such as Kom
Ombo, Edfu, and Esna, this time to complete the
surveying work and the drawings of the various
monuments.

Rosellini's *Journal* indicated March 8 as the date of
their arrival at Luxor, the eastern part of ancient
Thebes. With great enthusiasm all the members
began what they called "the Theban archaeological
campaign." However, Raddi had to go to the Delta,
since Grand Duke Leopold II had entrusted him with
gathering samples of local plants, minerals, and
animals.

While the mission was doing research on the
temple of Luxor, Rosellini found out that some locals
had discovered an intact tomb in the west necropolis
of Gurna. It was night. "When I got to the forum,"
Rosellini says in his *Journal*, "I entered the tomb,
which consisted of a small rock-cut vaulted chamber
that one had to bend way over to stand in . . . . Inside,

lying on the ground with their heads facing the entrance, were four mummy coffins. The first one, extraordinarily large, lay back against the left-hand wall and seemed to belong to a woman. The second was a man's coffin, then came the third, and lastly the fourth, housing a small body." All the mummies bore various amulets. At the time Rosellini wrote: "I bought the lot for thirty-two *thaler*s, plus a *bakshish* (tip) of sixteen piasters."

When the research on the famous archaeological site was finished, the mission went over to the western bank, in particular the Valley of the Kings, where they found comfortable lodgings in the tomb of Ramesses IV. The work of copying sculptures and hieroglyphic inscriptions was carried out for two months in about twenty tombs, including the stupendous tomb of Seti I, which had been discovered by Giovanni Battista Belzoni in 1817. Champollion and Rosellini removed two low reliefs from this tomb; they can now be seen at the Louvre in Paris and the National Archaeological Museum in Florence (see

Monumenti del Culto [Religious Monuments], plate LVIII).

Although finding a tomb intact was a rather rare occurrence, there was no end to the heated discussions with the workmen concerning the excavation itself: they were becoming more and more demanding, were not very painstaking, and often stole some of the objects they unearthed. Consequently, Champollion and Rosellini were obliged to suspend work temporarily and fire the laborers at their disposal.

The cook also left much to be desired. "The negligence he imparts to his tasks is unbearable," Rosellini notes with a bittersweet tone, "both in his uncleanliness and bad cooking. This evening (I had no lunch because I was indisposed) I ordered broth, which was excellent on other occasions. It had pigeon and chicken meat. The broth was not only insipid but downright undrinkable. I ordered a *cavás* (gendarme) to give him fifteen blows with a cane, which he did quite willingly, since he too was displeased with the cooking."

26 RIGHT
THE GOD HORUS
THEBES, TOMB OF SETI I
HISTORIC MONUMENTS, IV
PLATE CLV, DETAIL

A wall painting of the falcon-headed god Horus inside the tomb of Seti I, which Belzoni discovered in 1817.

26-27
DIVINITIES AND PHARAOHS
THEBAN TOMBS
HISTORIC MONUMENTS, IV
PLATE CXLVI, DETAIL

Polychrome illustrations of gods and sovereigns seen in the Ramesside tombs in the Valley of the Kings.

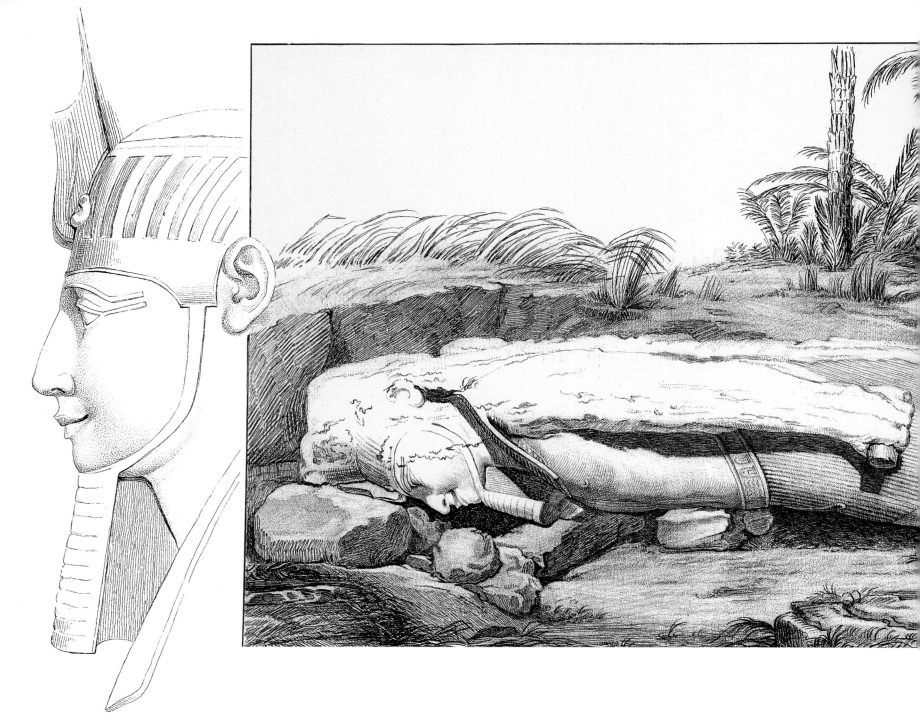

The research among the ruins of the Ramesseum
and Medinet Habu–further testimonies of two great
Ramessids–was carried out in torrid heat that was
particularly hard for the mission members to resist.
On August 7 they moved on to Karnak, on the
eastern bank, to explore the vast ruins of the great
temple of Amun.

Rosellini's travel journal ends with the date
August 9 and therefore did not contain the account
of the return trip from Thebes to Alexandria and
then on to Livorno. The Pisan scholar probably
thought it was better not to repeat the various
annotations and comments of a historical-
archaeological nature that he had already written
down in seven long letters sent from Egypt to his
colleagues in Pisa from August 1828 to June 1829.
However, as a finishing touch to his *Journal* there is a
long letter he sent in February 1830 to "dearest
Vieusseux," the director of the periodical *Antologia*,
in which Rosellini describes the immense ruins of
Karnak, the labor of copying of so many low reliefs,
and then the departure for Dendera, Cairo, and
Alexandria.

The arrival at Alexandria on September 23 had
been disturbed by the news of the death of Raddi

from dysentery on September 6, on the island of
Rhodes.

After being received by Mohammed Ali for their
leave-taking, the two Commissions decided to return
separately to their respective countries because the
Eglé, their ship, had not arrived. The Italian team left
on October 7 and Rosellini, his uncle Angelelli, and
Ricci finally reached Livorno in November, but had
to remain in quarantine until January 6, 1830.

Unfortunately, a few months after returning to
Italy, Alessandro Ricci's condition worsened because
of a scorpion bite, which triggered partial paralysis of
his body and mental disorder. The "excellent Dr.
Ricci," as Champollion used to call him, passed away
in 1834, with his inseparable friend Giuseppe
Angelelli at his bedside.

Champollion and Cherubini were the only French
members who left Egypt a month later, as the
illustrators stayed in Cairo to complete their work.

Thus, after fifteen months, the Franco-Tuscan
Expedition to the land of the pharaohs came to end,
not without some regrets, but above all with the
satisfaction of having achieved important scientific
results.

Rosellini had brought back to Italy about 1,400

illustrations, many of them in color, fourteen volumes of notes and hieroglyphic inscriptions, as well as about a thousand objects—most of them small—that had been either found or purchased in Egypt. Well aware of the value of this mission, which would certainly give a great boost to the burgeoning discipline of Egyptology, the Pisan scholar, with his characteristic honesty, could not but mention the passion and competence of his colleagues and express his gratitude to them: "I have been fortunate beyond all expectations to have had my Tuscan colleagues," he concluded, "to whom I owe the greatest part of the meager praise that may accrue to me from our undertaking."

But given the great recognition European scholars and various Italian and foreign academies heaped upon him, Rosellini deserved more than "meager praise." To conclude this memorial—and in doing so, taking up Gabrieli's thought—it is only right to say that for his total dedication to the study of the new discipline and his great virtues as a historian, philologist, and researcher, Rosellini deserves to stand alongside Champollion and Lepsius as one of the three founders of modern Egyptology.

The Monuments
of Egypt and Nubia
Pisa 1832-1844

Ippolito Rosellini

I MONUMENTI
DELL' EGITTO E DELLA NUBIA
ILLUSTRATI
DAL
PROF IPPOLITO ROSELLINI
Direttore della Spedizione Scientifico Letteraria
Toscana in Egitto
OPERA
Pubblicata sotto gli Auspicj
DI
S. A. I. e R.
IL GRAN-DUCA DI TOSCANA
etc. etc. etc.

LONDON:
H. HERING, 9 NEWMAN St.

*C*hampollion and Rosellini returned to their respective countries in early 1830 and saw each other again in the summer of the following year to carry out what they had planned: ". . . a work in common which, by producing great fruits for the science of antiquity, would honor France and Tuscany in equal measure . . . .".

As was mentioned above, the death of Champollion prevented their plan from being realized. Therefore, Rosellini, with his "Maestro" in mind, but also feeling his obligation to Grand Duke Leopold and science, threw himself headlong into the task of finishing "the long and fatiguing work" by himself. For eleven years, from 1832 until his death, Rosellini devoted all his energies to his work, struggling against numerous difficulties, not the least of which were illness and envious detractors.

The huge work is divided into three parts—Monumenti Storici ('Historic Monuments,' five volumes), Monumenti Civili ('Civil Monuments,' three volumes), and Monumenti del Culto ('Religious Monuments,' one volume)—and includes three in folio Atlases, one for each section. A French edition was published in 1835 with the same title, Monuments de l'Egypte et de la Nubie, but with somewhat different criteria.

Rosellini's volumes (the last of which was published posthumously)—which deal with the history of Egyptian civilization under the different ruling dynasties as well as the various aspects of its everyday life and religion—display great erudition and are an exemplary comment on the illustrations. The Atlases consist of 390 plates, 110 of which are in color. They are still an example of rare graphic excellence and help make Rosellini's work one of the most significant 'monuments' of Egyptology.

34 LEFT
KINGS AND QUEENS OF EGYPT
THEBES, VALLEY OF THE KINGS,
TOMB OF RAMESSES III
VOLUME II, PLATE XVI, DETAIL

In this plate, Ramesses III is depicted
wearing a splendid headdress with
the *atef* crown. The illustration was
copied from the pharaoh's tomb.

34 BOTTOM RIGHT
RULERS OF EGYPT
THEBES, VALLEY OF THE KINGS
VOLUME II, PLATE XVIII

This plate shows five pharaohs and
one prince (the last figure at bottom
right). Above, from left to right, are
portraits of Ramesses VII, Ramesses
IV, and Ramesses IX, who all
belonged to the Twentieth Dynasty.
Below, from left to right, are
Amenmesse (Nineteenth Dynasty),
Nectanebo I (Thirtieth Dynasty), and
one of Ramesses IX's sons. The splendid
colors bring out their rich attire.

Monuments

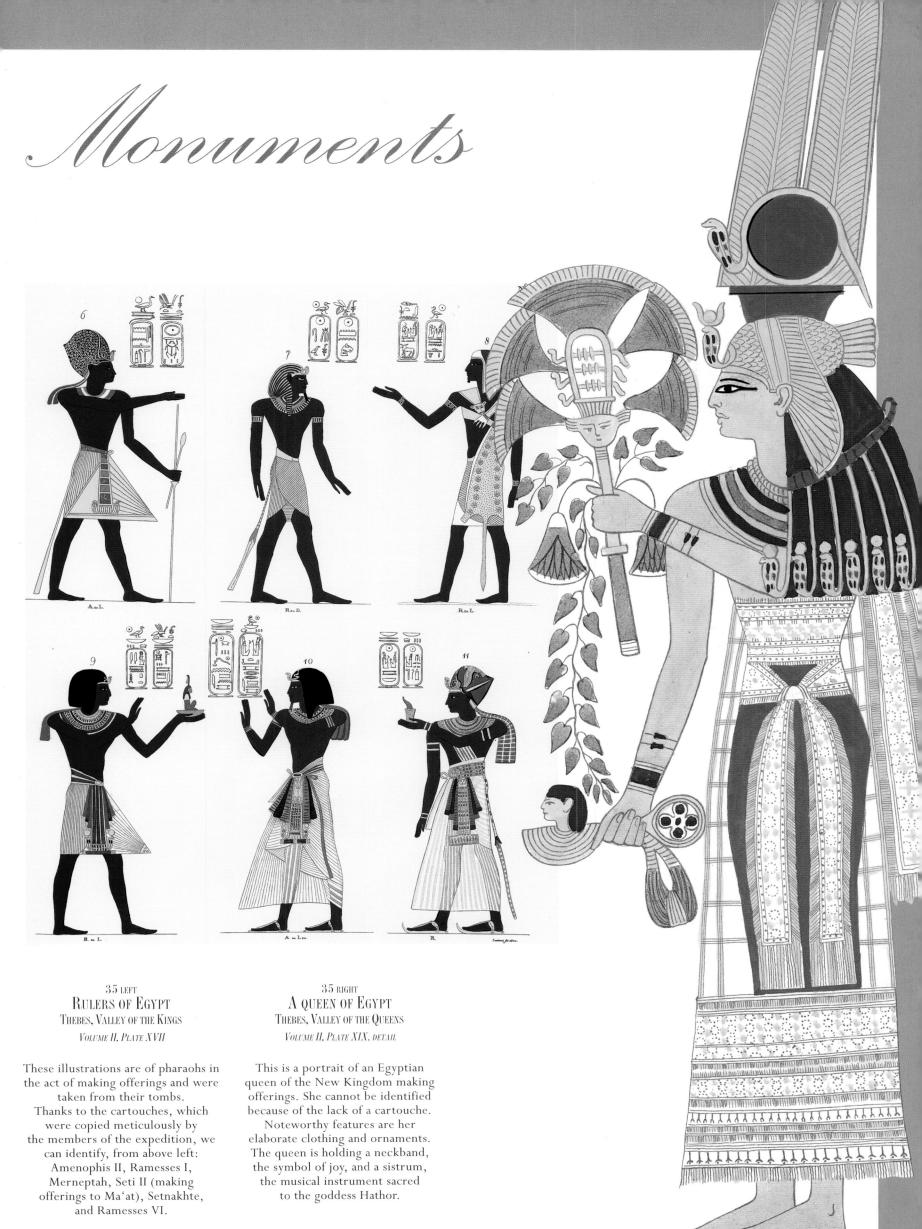

35 LEFT
RULERS OF EGYPT
THEBES, VALLEY OF THE KINGS
VOLUME II, PLATE XVII

35 RIGHT
A QUEEN OF EGYPT
THEBES, VALLEY OF THE QUEENS
VOLUME II, PLATE XIX, detail

These illustrations are of pharaohs in the act of making offerings and were taken from their tombs.
Thanks to the cartouches, which were copied meticulously by the members of the expedition, we can identify, from above left: Amenophis II, Ramesses I, Merneptah, Seti II (making offerings to Ma'at), Setnakhte, and Ramesses VI.

This is a portrait of an Egyptian queen of the New Kingdom making offerings. She cannot be identified because of the lack of a cartouche. Noteworthy features are her elaborate clothing and ornaments. The queen is holding a neckband, the symbol of joy, and a sistrum, the musical instrument sacred to the goddess Hathor.

36 TOP AND 37 TOP RIGHT

GROUP OF ASIATIC NOMADS
BENI HASAN, TOMB OF KHNUMHOTEP,
TWELFTH DYNASTY
VOLUME IV, PLATES XXVII AND XXVIII

The procession comprises thirteen figures, including women and children, as well as men with pointed beards and armed with bows, arrows, and cudgels. All of them have typical hooked noses and are wearing colorful clothes and sandals or leather footwear. The physiognomy, dress, bow, and the stringed instrument similar to the Greek lyre suggested to Champollion that these people were "Ionic Greeks or a people from Asia Minor . . . ."

36 BOTTOM AND 37 BOTTOM

GROUP OF ASIATIC NOMADS
BENI HASAN, TOMB OF KHNUMHOTEP,
TWELFTH DYNASTY
VOLUME IV, PLATE XXVI, DETAIL

One of the most interesting scenes in the main hall of this tomb is the one depicting the arrival in Egypt of a caravan of Bedouin from the eastern regions led by their chief, Abisha (seen below right), who is bowing respectfully while offering a pair of gazelles to the governor Khnumhotep (not depicted).

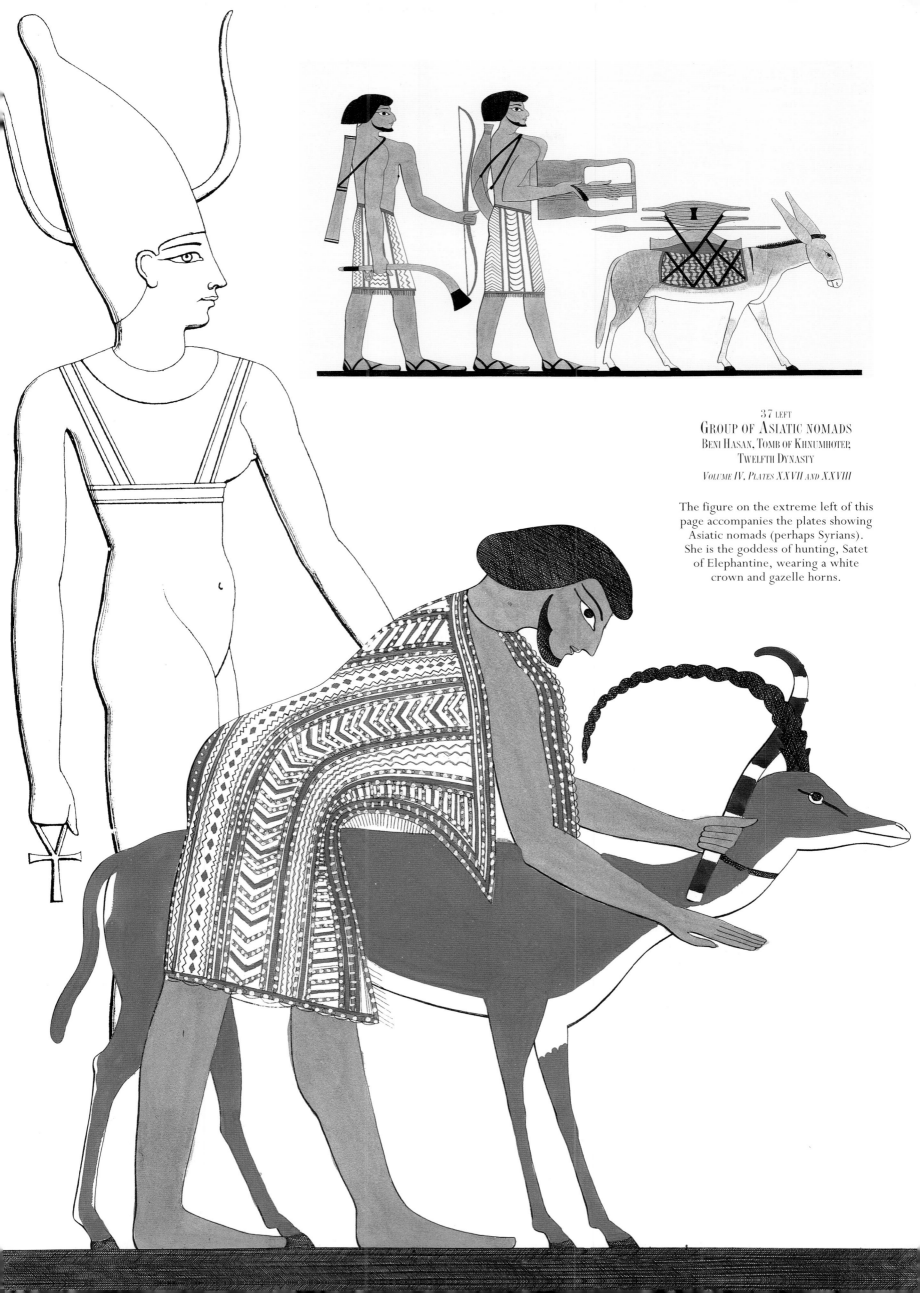

37 LEFT

GROUP OF ASIATIC NOMADS

BENI HASAN, TOMB OF KHNUMHOTEP,
TWELFTH DYNASTY

VOLUME IV, PLATES XXVII AND XXVIII

The figure on the extreme left of this
page accompanies the plates showing
Asiatic nomads (perhaps Syrians).
She is the goddess of hunting, Satet
of Elephantine, wearing a white
crown and gazelle horns.

THE MILITARY CAMPAIGNS OF RAMESSES II IN AFRICA
TEMPLE OF BEIT AL-WALI, NUBIA
VOLUME III, PLATE LXIV

The scene is set in the small Nubian temple dedicated to Amun-Ra that Ramesses II had built during his long reign. "Ramesses II strikes a black man, the emblem of the people of Cush [Ethiopians]" (Rosellini). Like other temples in Nubia, in the 1970s this one was dismantled, removed, and rebuilt about half a mile south of the Aswan High Dam so that it would not be flooded by the waters of Lake Nasser.

38-39
THE BATTLES AND VICTORIES OF RAMESSES II
ABU SIMBEL, GREAT TEMPLE
VOLUME III, PLATE LXXIX

This is the first of eight plates illustrating a series of scenes copied from the low reliefs in the pronaos of the rock-cut temple of Ramesses II. The pharaoh is depicted smiting a group of prisoners of different peoples in the presence of the god Amun-Ra, who in turn is offering the characteristic Egyptian sword to Ramesses.

THE BATTLES AND VICTORIES OF RAMESSES II
ABU SIMBEL, GREAT TEMPLE
VOLUME III, PLATE LXXX

A Syrian fortress on the top of a cliff is being attacked by the pharaoh. While the defenders are being killed by the Egyptian archers, a woman at the top of the fort is holding a child aloft to arouse the pharaoh's pity. Below, a Syrian flees with his herd.

41
THE BATTLES AND VICTORIES OF RAMESSES II
ABU SIMBEL, GREAT TEMPLE
VOLUME III, PLATE LXXXII

This is the last scene of the battle, depicting three princes, the pharaoh's sons, who can be identified by the lock of hair they wear at the side of their heads. They stand on their chariots, protected by the shield bearers; in one hand they hold a bow and, in the other, the reins of the horses elegantly decorated with multicolored materials.

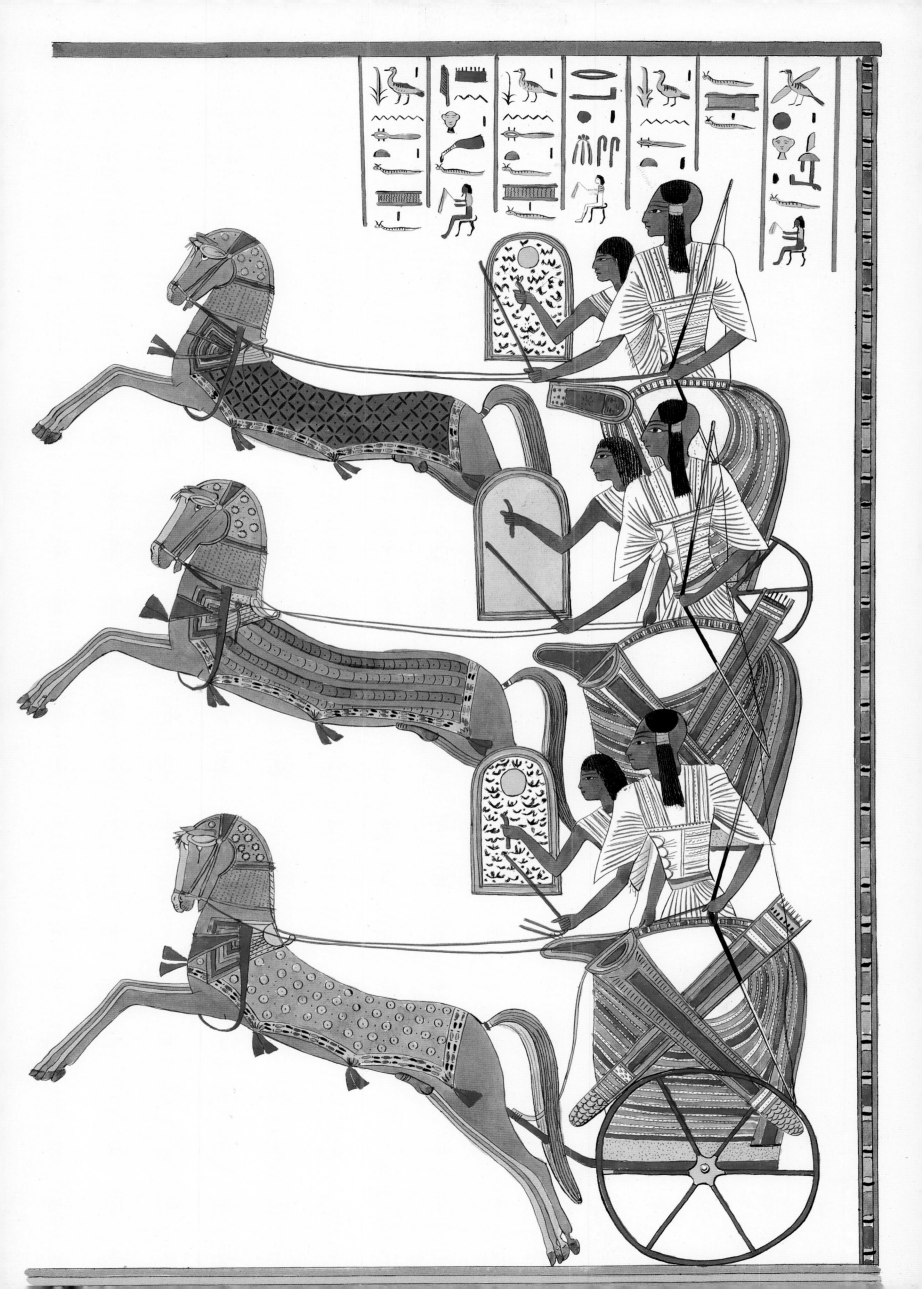

42-43
THE BATTLES AND VICTORIES OF RAMESSES II
ABU SIMBEL, GREAT TEMPLE
VOLUME III, PLATE LXXXIII

This plate and the following ones continue the self-glorification of the pharaoh. A recurring iconographic motif shows him crushing a hapless enemy leader and lancing another, both of whom are thought to be Libyans. Here the artist has ignored the canons of perspective and, in order not to cover Ramesses II's face, has rendered the lance in an unnatural manner so that it passes behind the head and left arm of the pharaoh.

43
THE BATTLES AND VICTORIES OF RAMESSES II
ABU SIMBEL, GREAT TEMPLE
VOLUME III, PLATE LXXXV

Here we have two groups of war prisoners, Ethiopians and Nubians. The prisoners wear animal skins and are bound by the neck and arms, who attest once again the famous ruler's victories over various African peoples. The gait of the figures (almost a mixture of dance steps) reveal how the Egyptian artists succeeded in lending a sense of movement to the entire scene.

44-45
VICTORIES OF RAMESSES II
ABU SIMBEL, GREAT TEMPLE
VOLUME III, PLATE LXXXIV

Taken from the south wall of the
pronaos, the scene depicts
the pharaoh in triumph.
Preceded by an archer, Ramesses II,

with a blue crown and a bow in his
left hand, is drawn in his war
chariot by a pair of elegantly
harnessed horses.

THE BATTLE OF KADESH
ABU SIMBEL, GREAT TEMPLE
VOLUME III, PLATE LXXXVII

This plate is a small-scale, summary reproduction of a large scene that covers the entire north wall of the pronaos in the temple at Abu Simbel.

It is divided into two parts. The upper register represents the pharaoh attacking a citadel near a river with his chariots. The lower one shows the army of chariots and foot soldiers in battle formation, the camp and the pharaoh's tent, the pharaoh in person receiving an ambassador and, lastly, a chariot battle.

This is the representation of the famous Battle of Kadesh, at the river Orontes in Syria, which Ramesses II fought against the Hittites around 1275 BC. In reality, neither side won the battle, but the ambitious Egyptian sovereign had the event propagandized as a sort of personal triumph.

47 BOTTOM LEFT
THE BATTLE OF KADESH
ABU SIMBEL, GREAT TEMPLE
VOLUME III, PLATE LXXXVII, DETAIL

This scene shows the perfectly aligned Egyptian footmen who are protected by chariots with archers and cuirassiers.

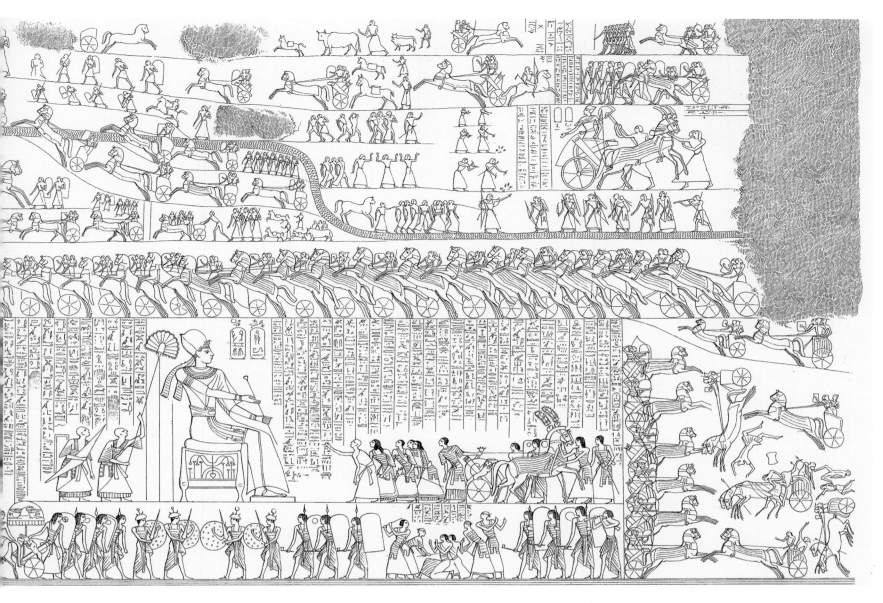

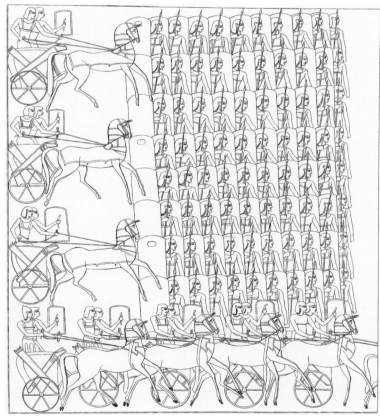

47 BOTTOM RIGHT
THE BATTLE OF KADESH
ABU SIMBEL, GREAT TEMPLE
VOLUME III, PLATE LXXXVII, detail

Ramesses II (right), shooting
an arrow from his chariot,
throws his enemies into disarray.

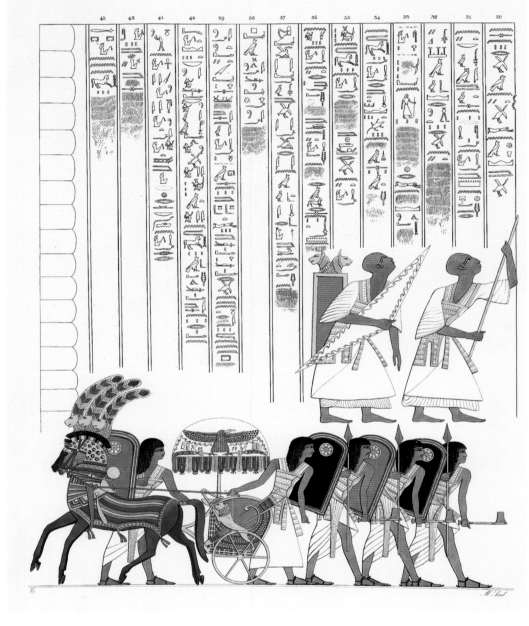

48 AND 49
THE BATTLE OF KADESH
ABU SIMBEL, GREAT TEMPLE
VOLUME III, PLATES C AND CI

The Battle of Kadesh, narrated in the
low reliefs in the Great Temple
of Abu Simbel, was copied
masterfully by the Franco-Tuscan
mission artists in January 1829.
Of the sixteen plates published in
Rosellini's work, in this page and
the following ones are reproductions
of the last four, which stand
out for their superb and
colorful images.

In the illustration at left, the pharaoh,
seated and in military dress, is being
informed of the enemy's imminent
attack. Below are the Egyptian forces,
among whom are various foreigners,
ready for battle. In the scene at right,
two servants (above) are holding
Ramesses II's flabellum and his bow
in its case; below are soldiers armed
with axes and lances, protected by
their breastplates. The long
hieroglyphic inscription contains
part of the so-called "Pentaur Poem,"
an account of the battle, which the
great pharaoh also had carved on the
walls of other temples.

THE BATTLE OF KADESH
ABU SIMBEL, GREAT TEMPLE
VOLUME III, PLATE CII

This plate is the conclusion of the preceding scene. Kneeling before Ramesses II (not portrayed), officers talk among themselves, while the servants try to calm down the horses. In the lower register, two Hittite spies are being beaten so that they will reveal the location of their army. Note the trumpeter among the Egyptian soldiers.

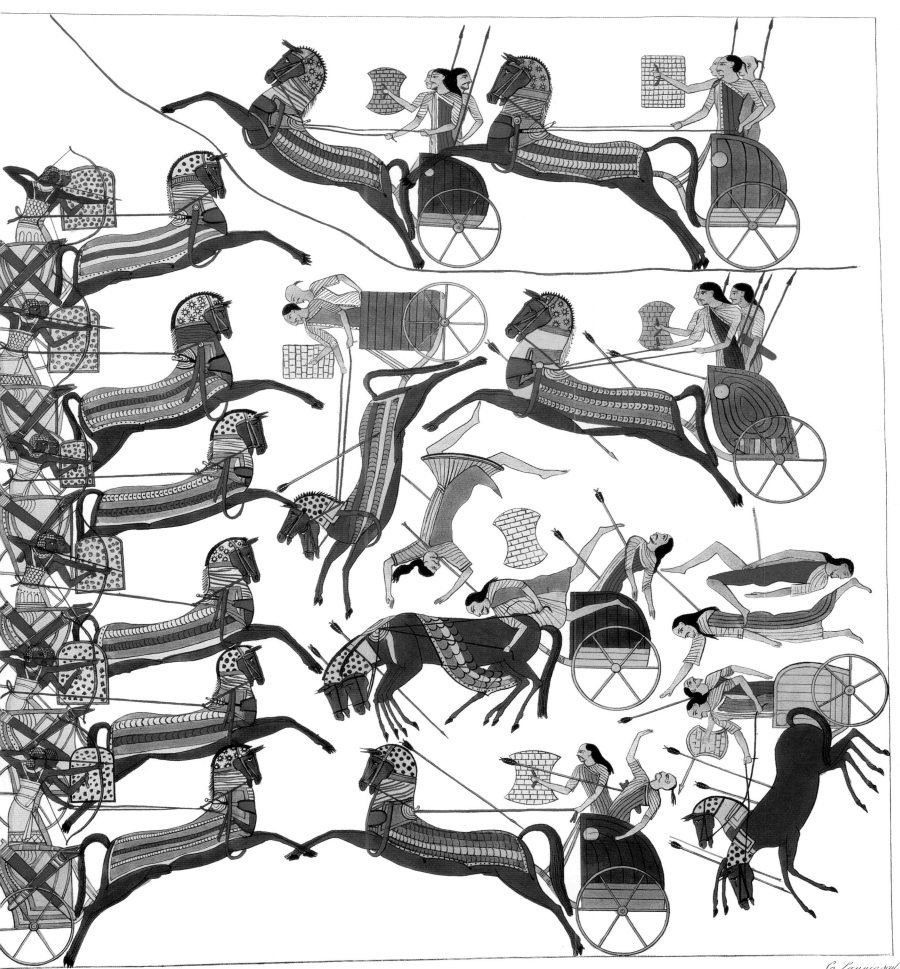

G. Lasinio scul.

THE BATTLE OF KADESH
ABU SIMBEL, GREAT TEMPLE
VOLUME III, PLATE CIII

This is the last of the sixteen plates
illustrating the famous event
immortalized in the Nubian temple.

Angelelli's beautiful polychrome
drawing shows, at left, the aligned
light Egyptian chariots with
two soldiers each. At right
are the heavier Hittite chariots,
which carry three soldiers; they are
fleeing, since both the soldiers
and horses have been struck by

Egyptian arrows. A typical feature
of Egyptian art is the lack of
perspective: the figures,
all of equal size, are 'staggered
vertically,' that is, one over
the other, and not on the same plane,
which lends a lack of depth
to the entire composition.

52-53
THE BATTLE OF KADESH
WEST THEBES, RAMESSEUM
VOLUME III, PLATE CIX

This is another representation
of the battle in Syria as it was
rendered in low relief on the right-
hand pylon of the funerary temple
of Ramesses II. Once again, in
keeping with classical Egyptian
iconographical canons, the pharaoh
is depicted on his chariot as he shoots
an arrow, while the battlefield
is covered with the bodies of the
dead and wounded enemy.

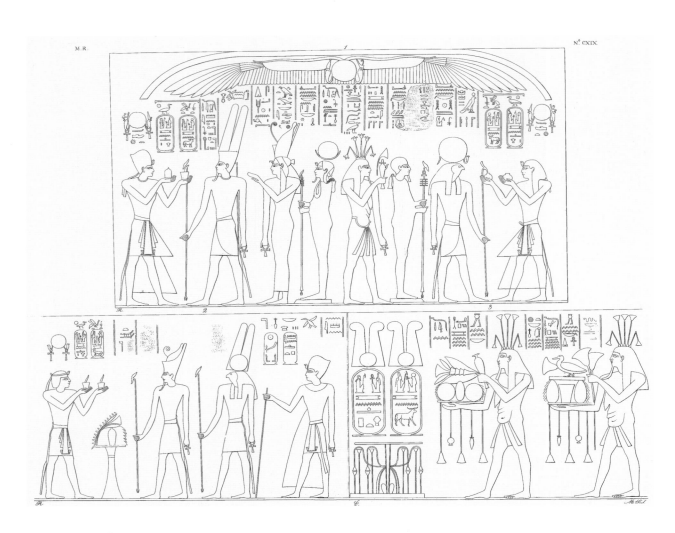

54 BOTTOM

HUNTING LIONS
MEDINET HABU, TEMPLE OF RAMESSES III
VOLUME III, PLATE CXXIX

Scenes of military prowess and courage are depicted in the temple that Ramesses III had built around 1200 BC. Besides showing a part of the Egyptian army, this plate illustrates the pharaoh hunting lions.

55

THE PHARAOH AND A GOD
THEBES, TOMB OF MERNEPTAH
VOLUME III, PLATE CXVIII

This plate shows the son of Ramesses II in splendid dress wearing the *atef* crown while receiving the gifts of stability and peace from the god Ra-Horakhty, the symbols of which are in his left and right hands.

54 TOP

THE PHARAOH MAKING OFFERINGS
THEBES, TOMB OF MERNEPTAH
VOLUME III, PLATE LXIX

On both sides of the image on the upper register, Merneptah, the son and successor of Ramesses II, is represented while offering vases of wine to various divinities. This act is repeated in the scene below left, while in the last scene the two symbolic personifications of the Nile seem to be taking gifts to the pharaoh's cartouche.

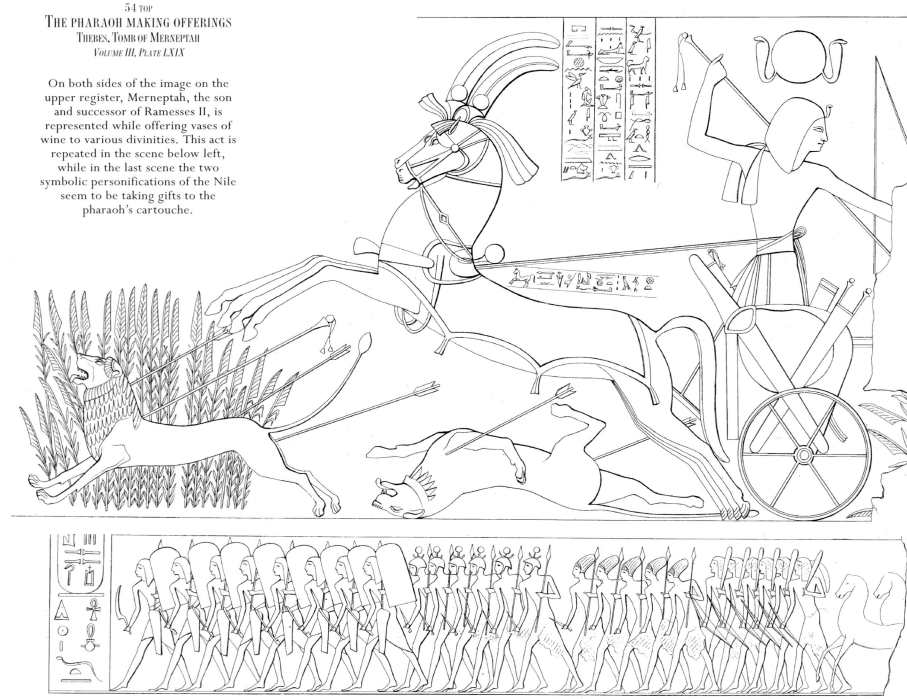

56-57
NAVAL BATTLE
MEDINET HABU, TEMPLE OF RAMESSES III
VOLUME III, PLATE CXXXI

This scene narrates the attempt to invade Egypt by the 'Sea Peoples,' populations from the Mediterranean and Asia Minor who were active in the region in the thirteenth-eleventh centuries BC. The are thought to have been Etruscans, Achaeans, Sardinians, and Lycians. Around 1180 BC, they were driven away by Ramesses III in a battle that may have been decisive for the independence of his country. The plate shows the Egyptians in battle on land and sea; their adversaries can be recognized by their feathered headdresses and round shields.

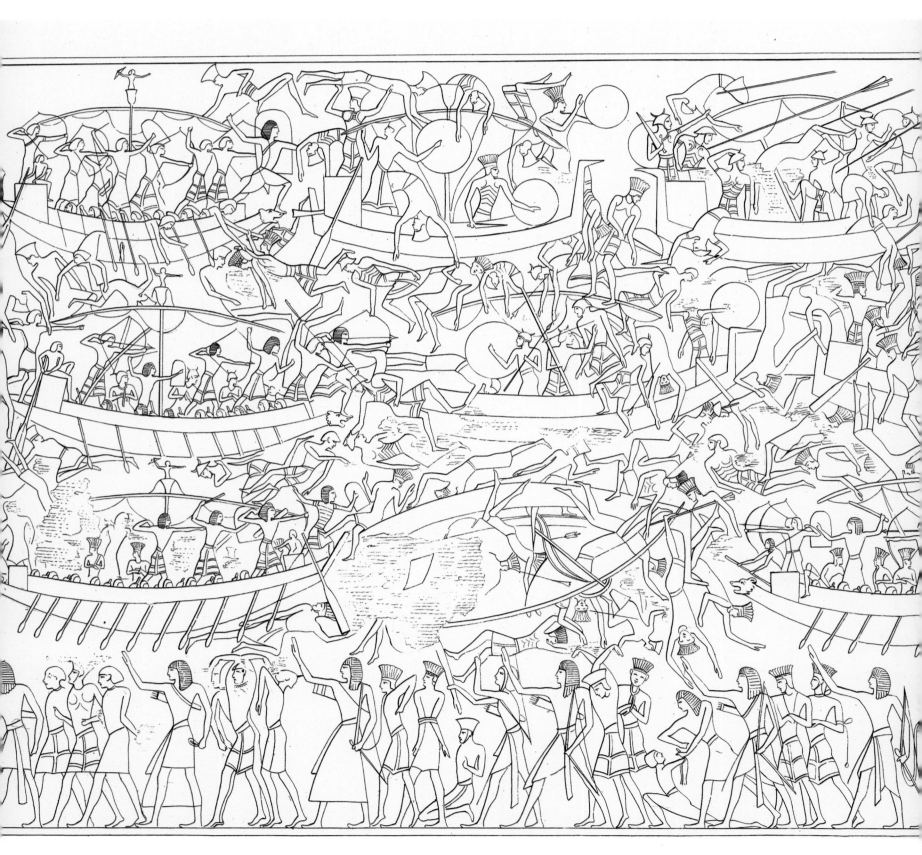

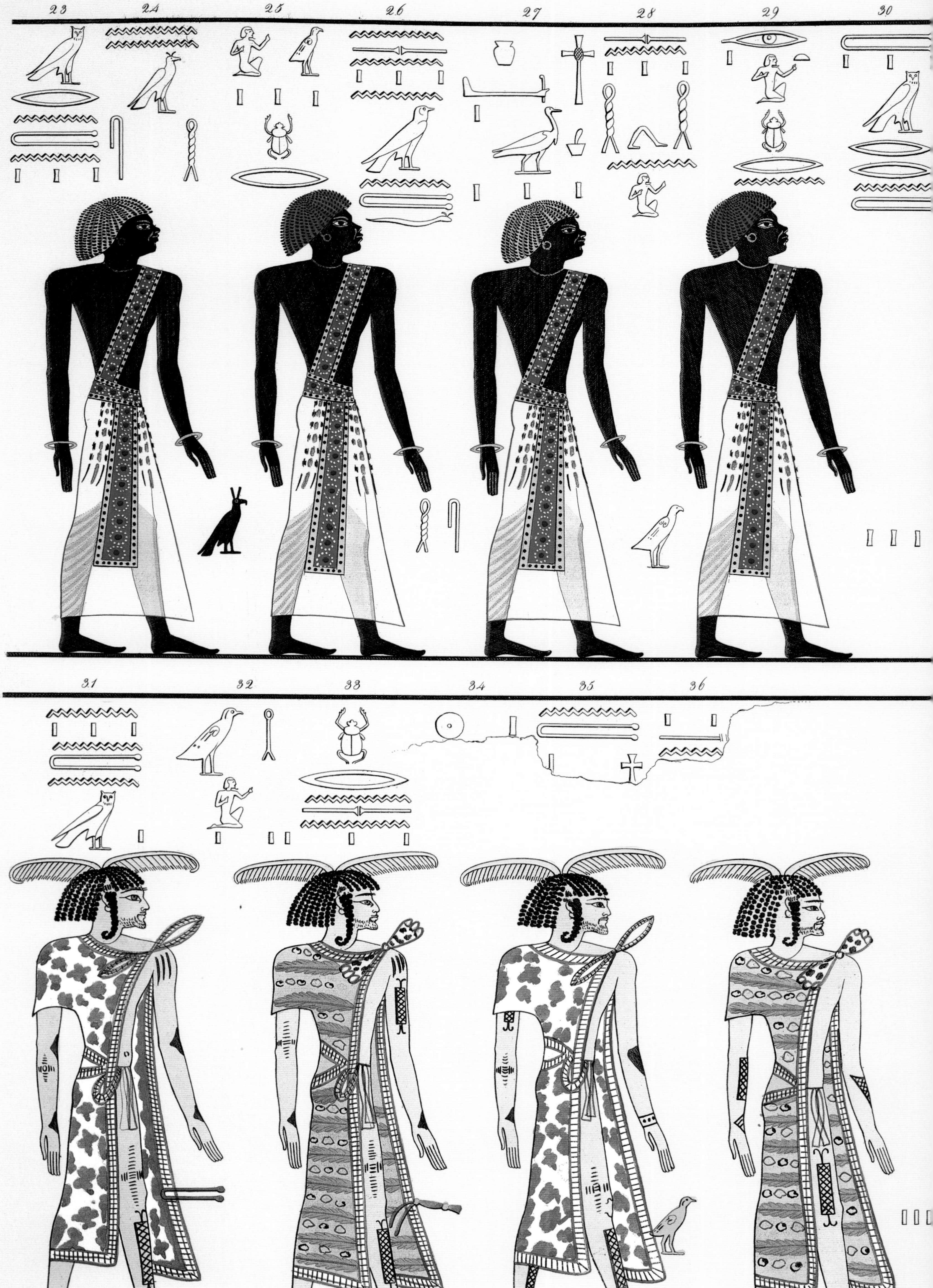

R... da B.

M. Scu

58
PROCESSION OF EGYPTIANS AND FOREIGNERS
THEBES, TOMB OF SETI I
VOLUME IV, PLATE CLVI

These are portrayals of representatives of some foreign populations who came into contact with the ancient Egyptians. The four Nubians in this upper section are easily recognizable: true black Africans with their dark skin and kinky hair, wearing long garments and bracelets on their wrists. Below are four other figures with light skin, straight noses, feathers in their hair and a sort of mantle wrapped around their left shoulder. They have been identified as Libyans.

59
PRISONERS OF WAR
WEST THEBES, RAMESSEUM
VOLUME III, PLATE CXLI

Two prisoners, an African and an Asian, on their knees with their necks and arms tied, represent another testimony to Ramesses II's victories.

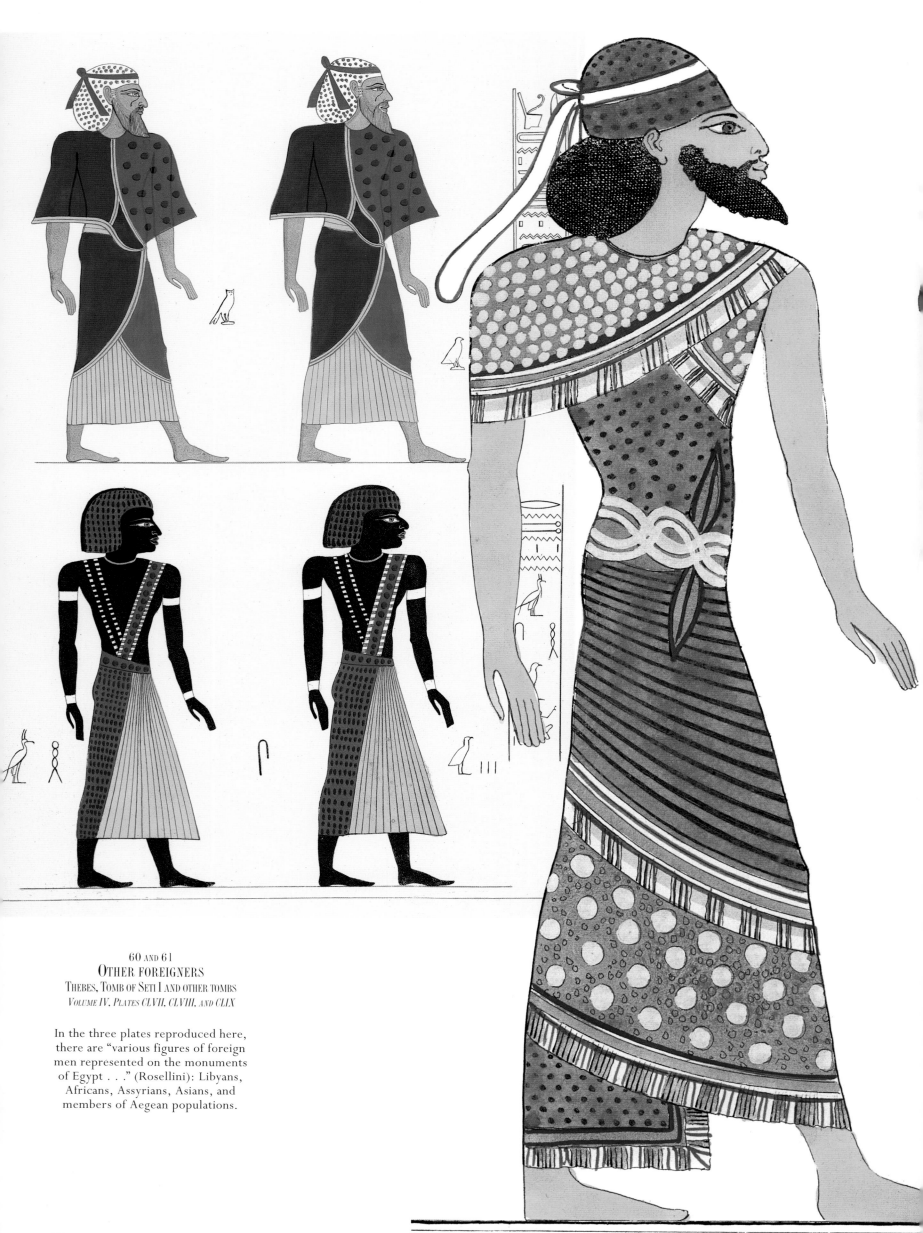

60 AND 61
OTHER FOREIGNERS
THEBES, TOMB OF SETI I AND OTHER TOMBS
VOLUME IV, PLATES CLVII, CLVIII, AND CLIX

In the three plates reproduced here, there are "various figures of foreign men represented on the monuments of Egypt . . ." (Rosellini): Libyans, Africans, Assyrians, Asians, and members of Aegean populations.

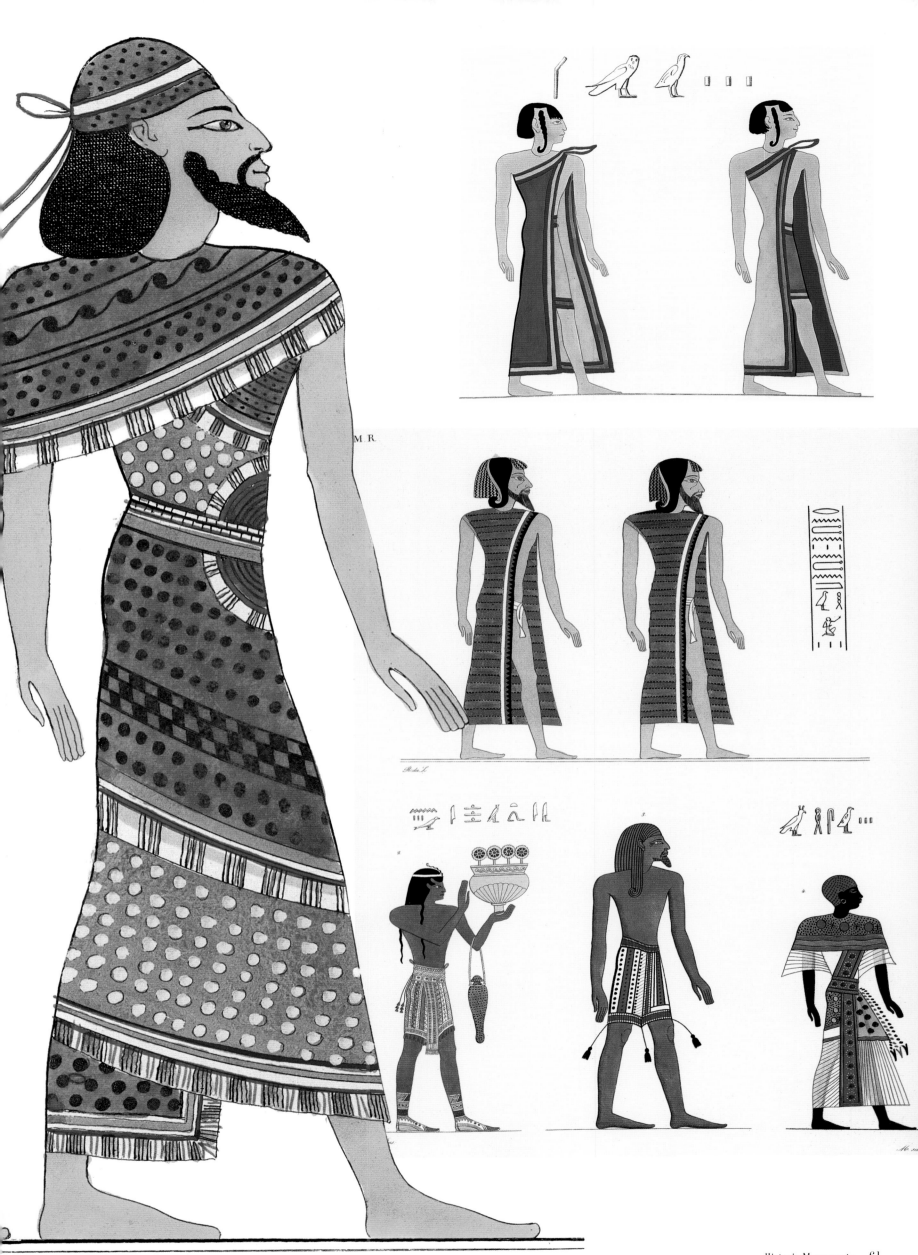

M.R.

62-63
HEADS OF FOREIGNERS
ABU SIMBEL AND THE TOMB OF SETI I
VOLUME IV, PLATE CLX

The plate is a synthesis of the physical features of some ethnic groups already described above. They include the heads of three Asians (figures 1, 2, 3), one Libyan (figure 4), and a Nubian (figure 5).

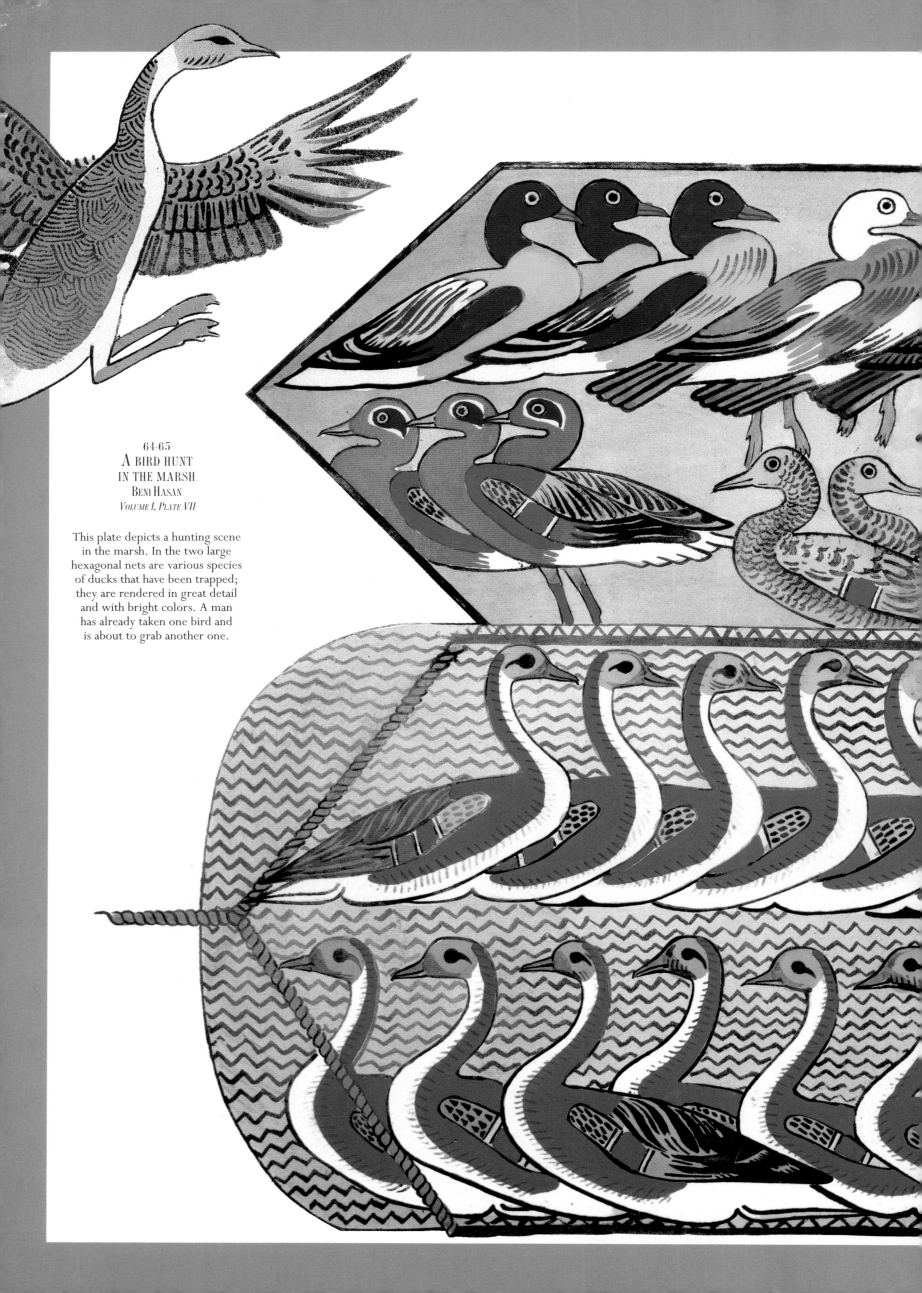

64-65
A BIRD HUNT IN THE MARSH
BENI HASAN
VOLUME I, PLATE VII

This plate depicts a hunting scene
in the marsh. In the two large
hexagonal nets are various species
of ducks that have been trapped;
they are rendered in great detail
and with bright colors. A man
has already taken one bird and
is about to grab another one.

66 TOP
VARIOUS SPECIES
OF EXOTIC ANIMALS
Thebes, Tomb of the vizier Rekhmira
Volume I, Plate XXII

The animals depicted here are
quadrupeds not native to Egypt,
and are for the most part associated
with foreigners who are perhaps
in the act of bearing tributes.
From above left: a giraffe with a cute
monkey on his neck, is tied down
by two Nubians; a lion with particular
markings, a bear-like animal
(figure 5) and a small elephant
(figure 3) are being led by what appear
to be Syrians, given their attire
and beards. In the middle is an
Ethiopian holding either a leopard
or a cheetah by a leash and carrying
a trunk of highly prized ebony
on his shoulders.

66-67 BOTTOM
VARIOUS SPECIES OF QUADRUPEDS
Beni Hasan
Volume I, Plate XX

From left to right are a dog with a spiral
tail, an Asian bull with a large lotus-
shaped collar, and a small carnivore
climbing up a papyrus plant. This last
animal was widespread in ancient Egypt
and was called *Viverra zibetta* (a species
of civet cat) by Rosellini.

67 top
Fantastic Animals
Beni Hasan and a Theban tomb
Volume I, Plate XXIII

Besides a greyhound and a cheetah (figures 1 and 3), which Rosellini calls a "hunter tiger," this illustration has some species of chimeras or griffins, which are probably the fruit of the tomb painters' imaginations.

68 top
VARIOUS SPECIES
OF AQUATIC BIRDS
Beni Hasan, Tomb of Khnumhotep
VOLUME I, PLATE XIII

Some species of ducks and geese are
rendered quite accurately and in
detail. There are also two ibises,
which were considered sacred by
the ancient Egyptians.

68 bottom and 69 bottom
Various species of birds
Beni Hasan
Volume I, Plate XI

These illustrations, once again copied from a tomb at Beni Hasan, depict other species of birds, most of which are aquatic, rendered with bright colors, among which a splendid heron on a flower stands out.

68-69 top
Various species of birds
Beni Hasan, Tomb of Khnumhotep
Volume I, Plate VIII

The charming birds illustrated here are also depicted with lovely colors. Among them are a hoopoe and a shrike perched on a small branch of a Nilotic mimosa, and a jay in flight.

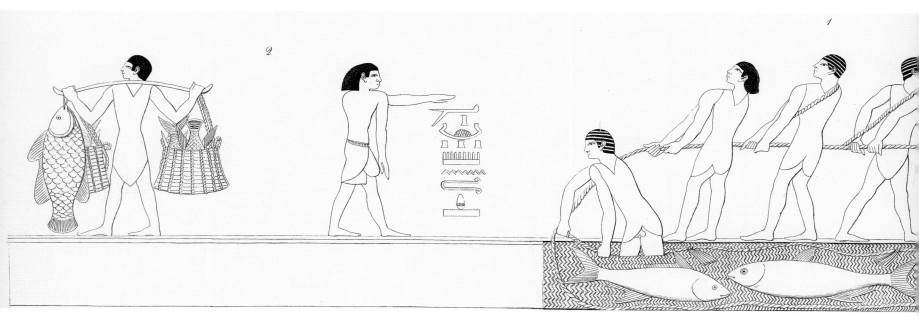

70-71 TOP
FISHING
BENI HASAN
VOLUME I, PLATE XXV

This plate features a scene of spear fishing and representations of various species of fish, all drawn in detail and with subtle color nuances. Above right, a man is cutting a fish and preparing it to be preserved.

70-71 BOTTOM AND 71
FISHING SCENES
BENI HASAN AND KOM AL-AHMAR
VOLUME I, PLATE XXIV

Different Egyptian fishing techniques are illustrated here. In the pictures copied from the walls of the Beni Hasan tombs, some men are fishing from the shore with a trawl net and others with a hook and line, while the scene at top right, copied from a tomb at Kom al-Ahmar, illustrates the use of a harpoon to catch crocodiles from a typical papyrus boat.

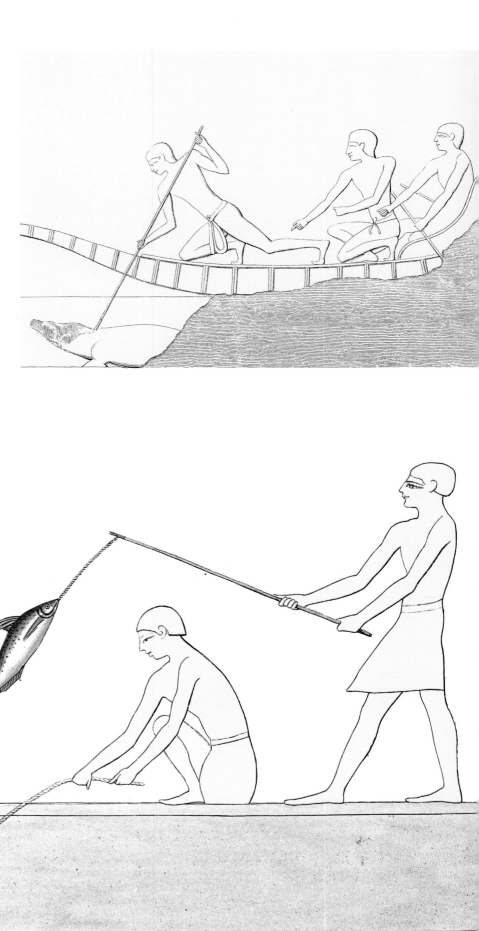

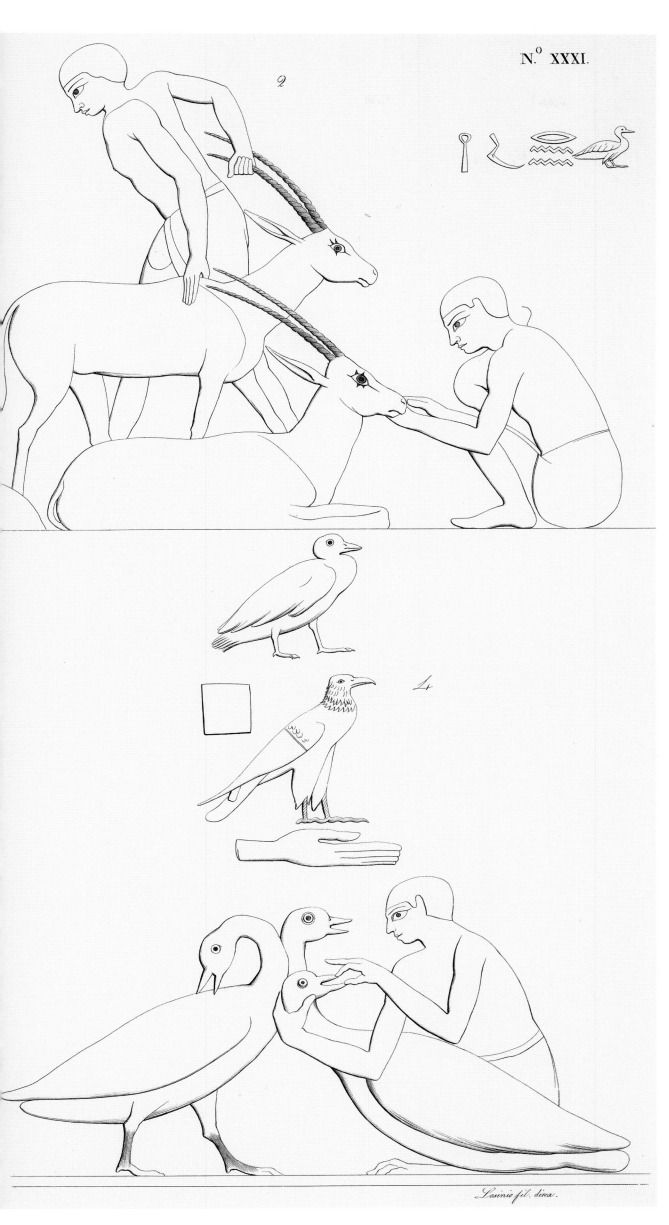

72-73
LIVESTOCK RAISING
BENI HASAN
VOLUME I, PLATE XXXI

Although Rosellini considered this a "veterinarian" scene, it more likely depicts the forced feeding of animals. In effect, the men seem to be forcefully putting food in the mouths of the oxen, gazelles, goats, and geese.

74-75
WINE-MAKING SCENES
GIZA, BENI HASAN, AND THEBES
CIVIL MONUMENTS, PLATE XXXVII

Viniculture in Egypt was carried out in very ancient times and developed mostly in the Nile Delta. Wine was drunk almost exclusively by the upper classes, while beer, made mostly from barley, was very widespread and was always on the tables of common people. After the harvest, the grapes were trodden; in order not to slip in the vat, the men shown here are holding on to a support. More pressing was then done with the aid of a bag. The juice dripped into a tub and was then poured in earthen amphorae to age. The ancient Egyptians wrote the quantity as well as the provenance, the name of the landowner, and the vintage year on the amphorae–much like a modern-day wine label. A scribe, with a quill behind his ear, is noting down the amount of wine.

74 LEFT AND BOTTOM
FARM SCENES
BENI HASAN AND AL-KAB
VOLUME I, PLATE XXXIV

The various phases of the wheat harvest included winnowing, measuring, transporting, and storing wheat under the watchful gaze of the scribe (center). Below, the grain is transported and then preserved in a two-story silo with several compartments, on each of which the harvest yield is indicated.

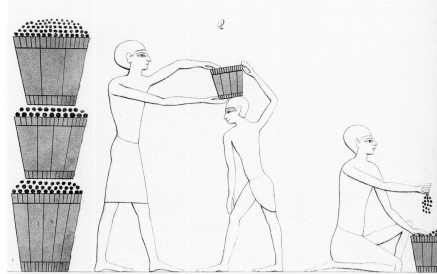

75 BOTTOM
FARM SCENES
BENI HASAN AND THE THEBES AREA
PLATE XXXVI, DETAIL

The upper scene depicts, from left to right: flax being harvested, and durra, a grain sorghum used as food, being cut and then transported. The lower scene shows the threshing of the harvest carried out by oxen, as well as two men who have just cut a number of papyrus stems. The fibers of this plant were used, among other things, for making writing material.

76-77
CULTIVATION AND IRRIGATION
BENI HASAN
VOLUME I, PLATE XL

This plate illustrates the two most common methods of irrigating crops and gardens in ancient Egypt. The manual system, consisting of people carrying vessels filled with water on their shoulders and then pouring the water into the different plots of land is illustrated above; below, the mechanical system, which made use of the *shaduf*, a suspended rod with a weight at one end and a bucket at the other which was used to raise water from the Nile or the many canals. The plate also has drawings of vegetables and fruit, as well as a date palm.

76 BOTTOM
FARMING
VARIOUS TOMBS
VOLUME I, PLATE XXXII, DETAIL

This scene, which is probably taking place in a field along a canal, depicts plowing, which in ancient Egypt was carried out with the aid of oxen. The scene continues with a farmer sowing the newly plowed land.

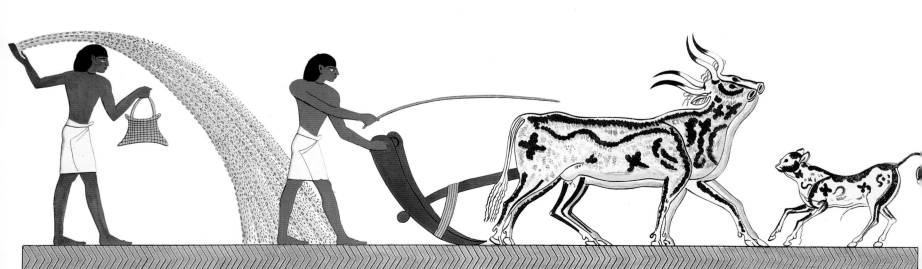

This charming scene depicts figs being picked by two people while monkeys are absorbed in eating the sweet fruit. According to Rosellini, in the other scene these peasants are gathering okra, an edible vegetable of the hibiscus family.

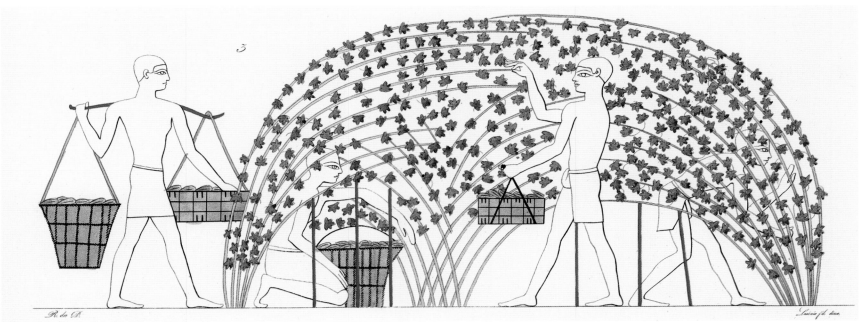

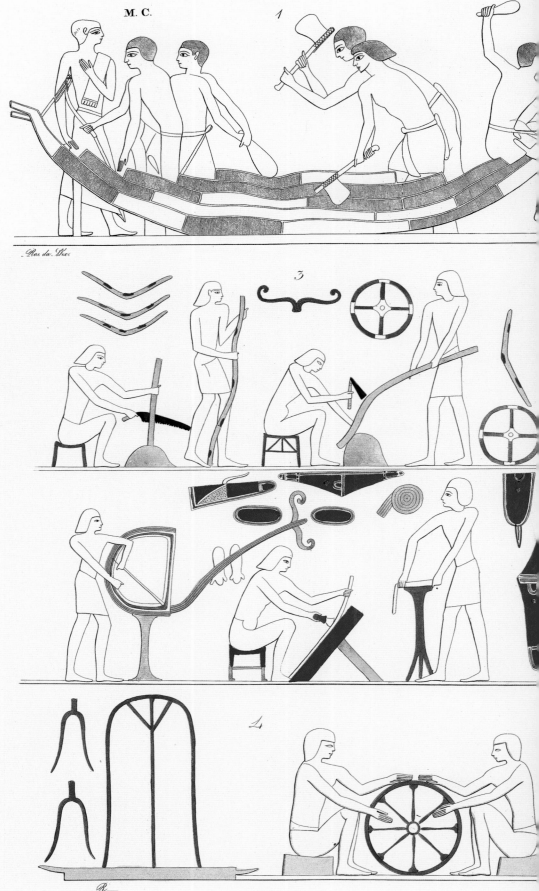

78 top and bottom, **79** right and bottom
Spinning and Weaving
Volume II, Plate XLI, detail

The only fiber worked by the ancient
Egyptians to produce fabrics was
flax, which had been used since the
Neolithic era. The first two registers
(bottom left) show the different
phases of soaking the flax, beating
it with wooden mallets, and preparing
the yarn. In the third and fourth
registers (next page, bottom),
some men are weaving on horizontal
looms, while in the last scene
(top right) two women are working
with a vertical loom.

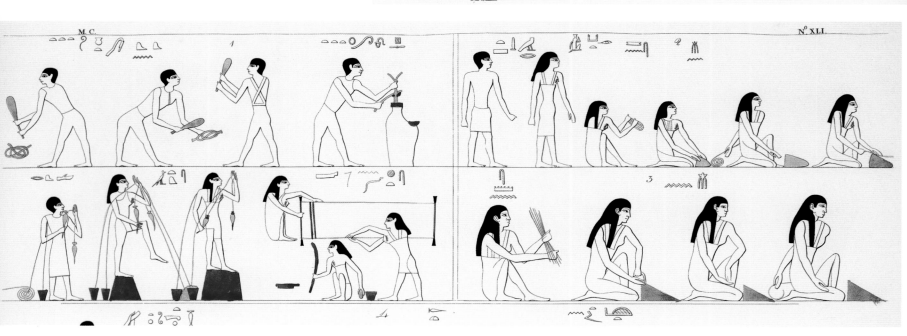

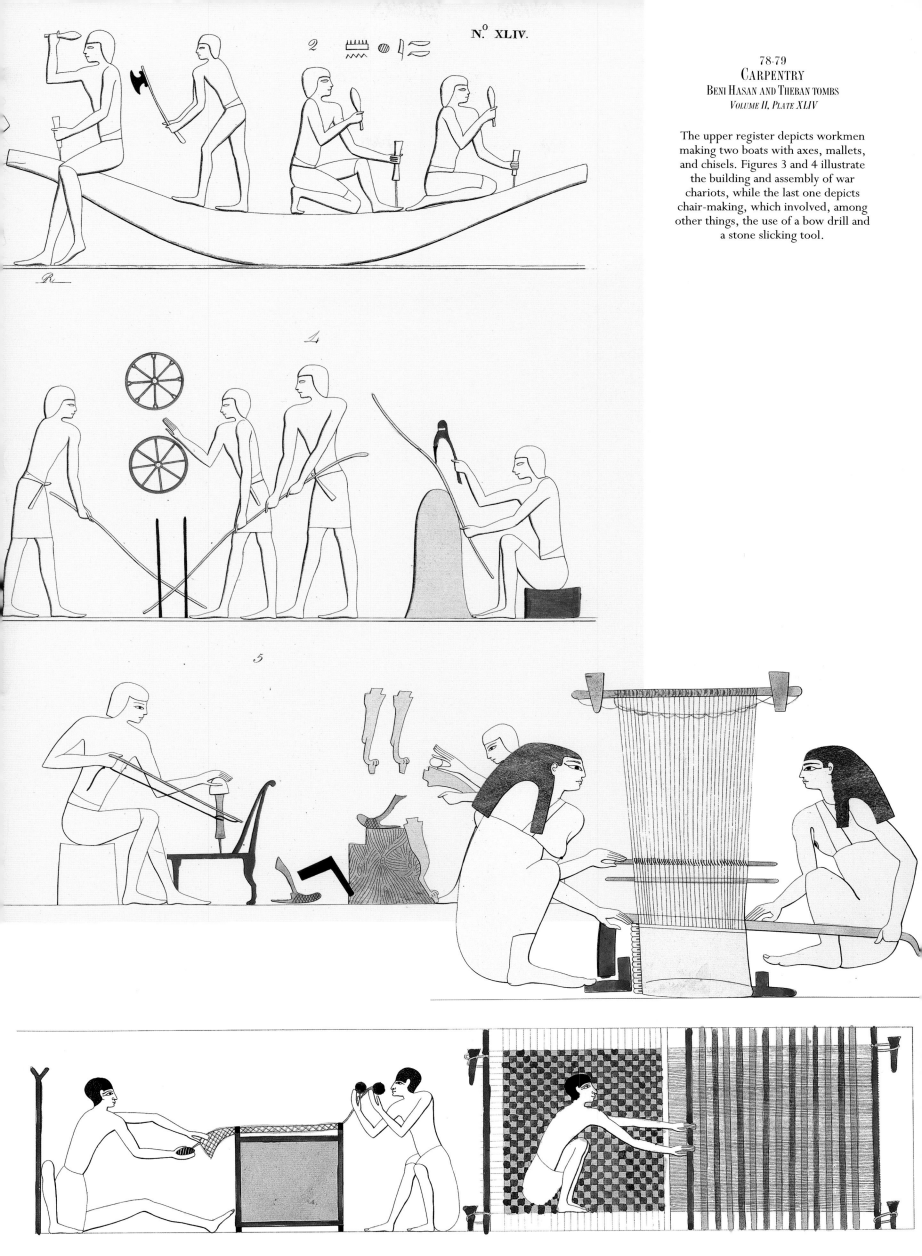

78-79
CARPENTRY
BENI HASAN AND THEBAN TOMBS
VOLUME II, PLATE XLIV

The upper register depicts workmen making two boats with axes, mallets, and chisels. Figures 3 and 4 illustrate the building and assembly of war chariots, while the last one depicts chair-making, which involved, among other things, the use of a bow drill and a stone slicking tool.

80-81
THE ART OF SCULPTING
THEBAN TOMBS, INCLUDING THE TOMB OF REKHMIRA
VOLUME II, PLATE XLVII

The plate first illustrates the art of sculpting a statue of a lion and a sphinx (figures on the left). This is followed by several artisans giving the final touches to two large red granite statues representing a standing pharaoh and a pharaoh on his throne (from Rekhmira's tomb in Thebes). The scenes below illustrate the transport of a wooden trunk and a block of stone.

80 BOTTOM
TRANSPORTING A COLOSSUS
TOMBS IN MIDDLE EGYPT
VOLUME II, PLATE XLVIII, detail

This plate shows a famous scene taken from a tomb in Deir al-Bersha. A huge statue is being transported: it is tied to a sledge and dragged by eight rows of men. The person on the colossus' knee is beating time with his hands in order to synchronize the movement of the laborers. One workman is pouring water on the sand so that the sledge will slide better, while below him three water bearers stand ready to help him.

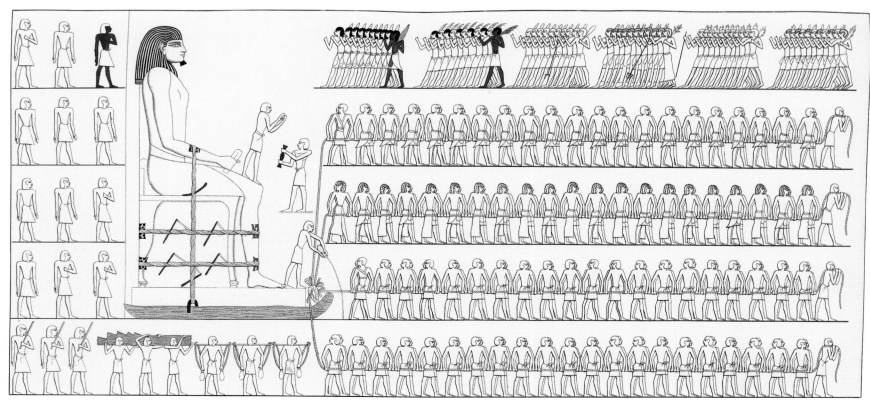

81 TOP
CARPENTRY
BENI HASAN AND THEBAN TOMBS
VOLUME II, PLATE XLV

The upper register depicts artisans making furniture and various wooden objects, including a chest, a bed, and a casket. The illustration in the middle shows the construction of a wooden papyrus column, while the other drawings are of models of religious and mortuary decorative art, such as mummiform statues, canopic jars, a *djed* pilaster, and a sphinx presenting offerings.

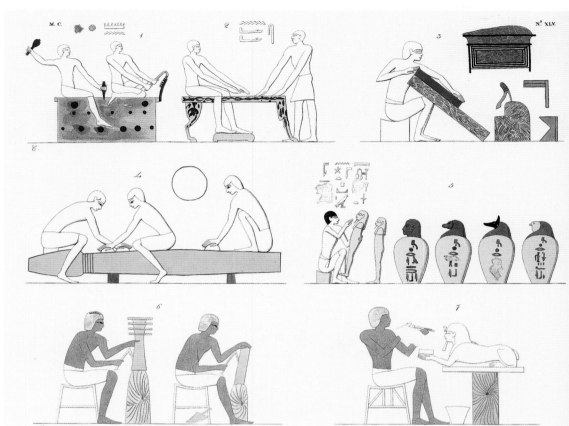

81 CENTER AND BOTTOM
DYERS AND PAINTERS
BENI HASAN AND THEBAN TOMBS
VOLUME II, PLATE XLVI

The upper register has three scenes depicting the grinding and preparation of colors, and then decorators varnishing wooden caskets.
The scenes in the lower register depict examples of sculpting, which involved the use of chisels and mallets as well as polishing and decorating the pieces with ornaments.

MASONRY
Thebes, Tomb of Rekhmira
Volume II, Plate XLIX

The scenes above and below left illustrate the process of making mud bricks in rectangular molds and then transporting them: note the darker color of the dried bricks compared to those just molded. Figures on the right show painters and sculptors working on vases and statues. The different physical features—such as the color of the skin, the beard, and the hair—led Rosellini to think the workmen were Jews, but it is more likely that they were Syrians.

82 bottom and 83 bottom, 83 top right

METALLURGY
Beni Hasan and Thebes
Volume II, Plate L

In these illustrations, which are copies of decorations in an Eighteenth Dynasty Theban tomb, we see phases of the melting and filtering of gold, which was mined in Nubia and the eastern zone of Egypt. Using foot-operated bellows, the artisans stoke the fire, melt the gold, and pour it into small receptacles of the same size. The scene at top right, from a tomb at Beni Hasan, depicts potters at work: after kneading the clay with their feet, they then shaped the vessels at the potter's wheel, fired them in cylindrical ovens, and transported them. Terracotta was the most common material used for pottery, but the ancient Egyptians also used stones such as limestone, granite, and alabaster.

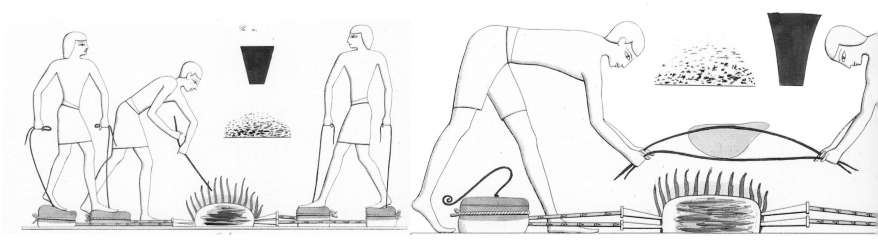

84 top
OTHER TYPES OF VASES
THEBAN TOMBS AND BENI HASAN
Volume II, Plate LX

In this plate are illustrated vases and
vessels with different shapes. They are
made of enamel, gold, and other
materials and sometimes have supports
beneath them. The drawing below
depicts three unusual small vases
decorated with lotus flowers.

84 bottom right
VASES AND DIFFERENT VESSELS
THEBAN TOMBS
Volume II, Plate LXII, detail

Here we have more illustrations
of vases and other vessels that
are finely decorated with depictions
of lotus and papyrus flowers.
The objects were made of precious
or semiprecious metal that was
enameled or gilded.

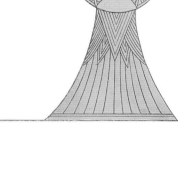

85
GOLDEN VASES
THEBES, TOMB OF NEBAMUN
Volume II, Plate LVIII

Different types of amphorae and vases
"of gold and enamel" (Rosellini) are
illustrated here. All of them are
elaborately decorated and have handles
and lids depicting animals or gods.
These extremely elegant objects
"preceded the beautiful production of
Greek art by a thousand years"
(Champollion).

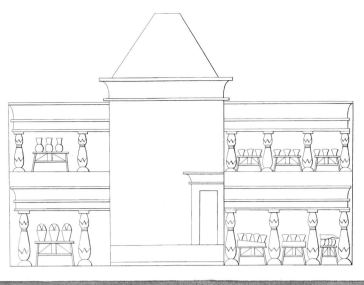

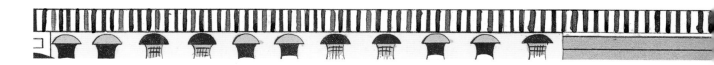

86-87
SCENES OF DOMESTIC LIFE
THEBAN TOMB
VOLUME II, PLATE LXVIII

Here is Rosellini's description of this scene: "The exterior of a house" (top figure) and "Inner courtyard of a house with garden, where a feast is taking place" (left figure). The owner is entering with his two children and a maidservant, preceded by some women and a man bearing food and fresh water (bottom left). A large amount of food and drink is seen in the middle of the scene, which may be a rather uncommon example from private life in ancient Egypt.

Lasinio f. dir.

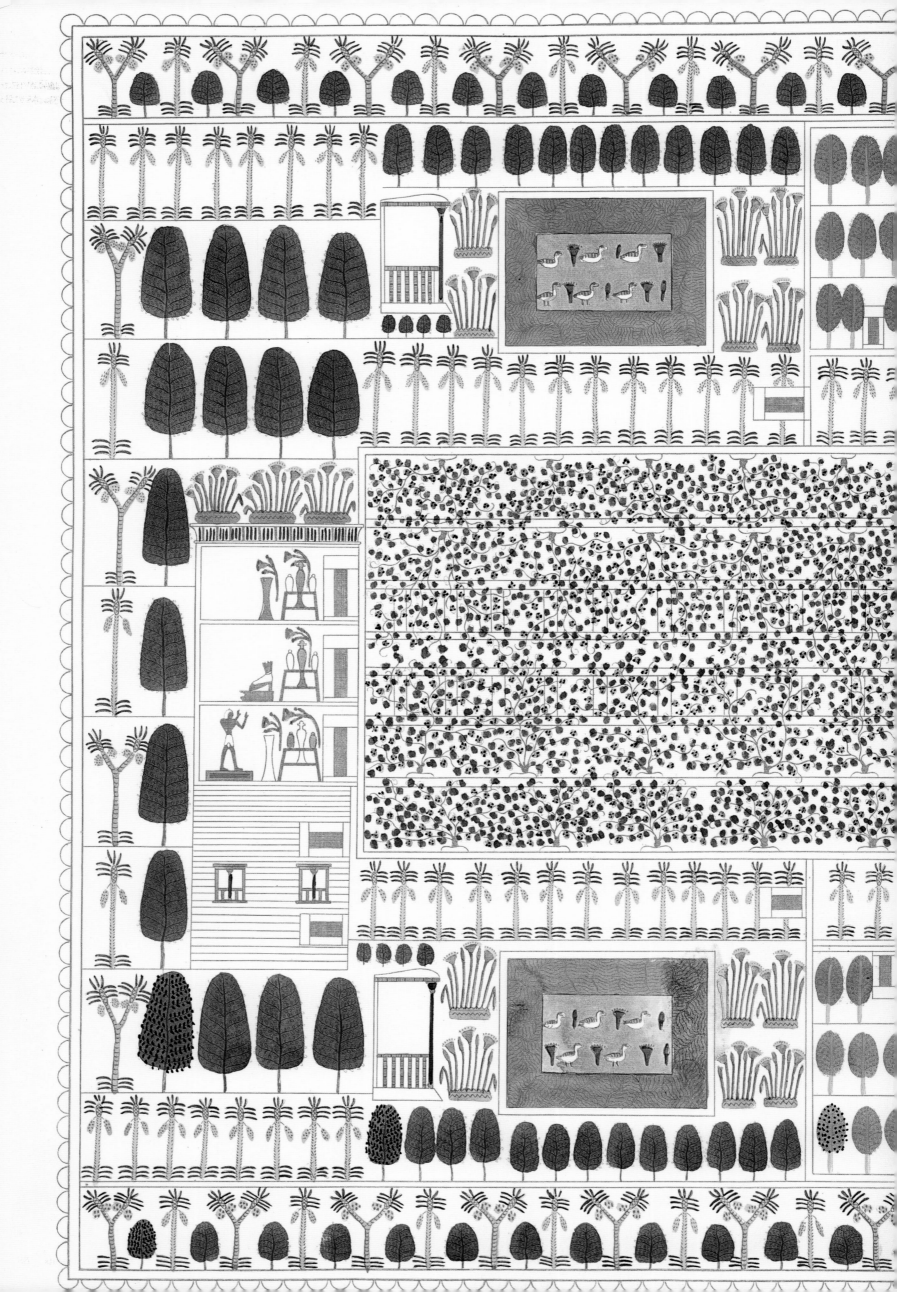

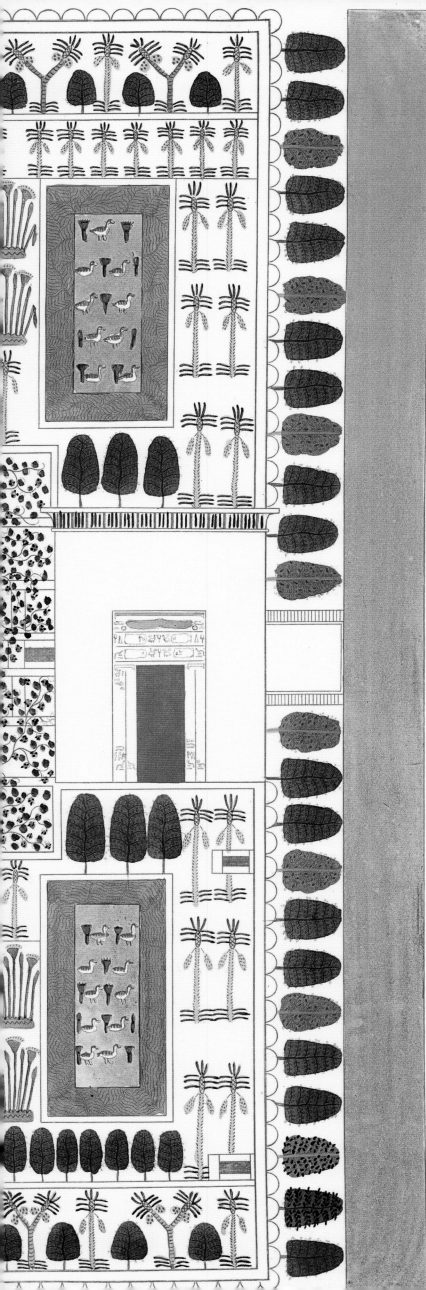

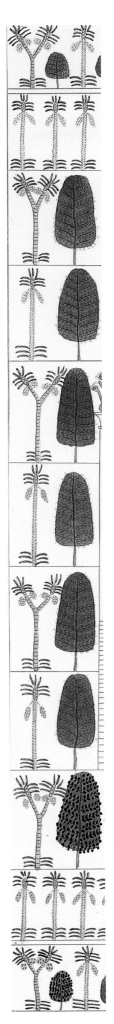

A GARDEN
THEBAN TOMB
VOLUME II, PLATE LXIX

This scene is the only evidence
of what remains of the 'Garden
of Amun,' which was drawn in a
nobleman's tomb. In fact, the scene
no longer exists, because it was
either removed or destroyed after the
Franco-Tuscan expedition.
The entire garden is illustrated
with plan and elevation drawings, in
keeping with the particular canons
of Egyptian painting. In the middle
is a vineyard, while all around there
are paths lined with palm and
sycamore trees. Papyrus plants and
pools in which ducks are swimming
elegantly round off this bucolic scene.

This plate has examples of polychrome decoration and ornaments on the walls and ceilings of tombs, royal palaces, and private mansions. Besides the geometric and plant motifs, there is a marked preference for stylized plants or flowers. The spiral shown above and in the middle, on the other hand, is a feature typical of the Aegean civilization and was adopted by Egyptian art in the Middle Kingdom. Note the motif of the star-studded ceiling so common to many tombs.

M.C.

Here are other examples of friezes and decoration on the vaults and floors of tombs, temples, and private houses. The latter were often decorated with checkered geometric motifs or with birds in flight. The different motifs drew inspiration from the patterns on the fabric usually used to conceal the beams that supported the ceilings in patrician houses.

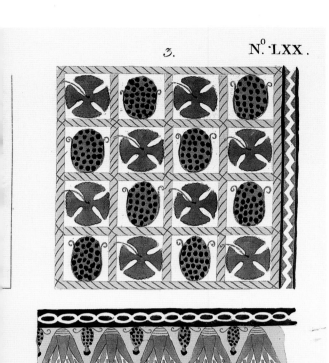

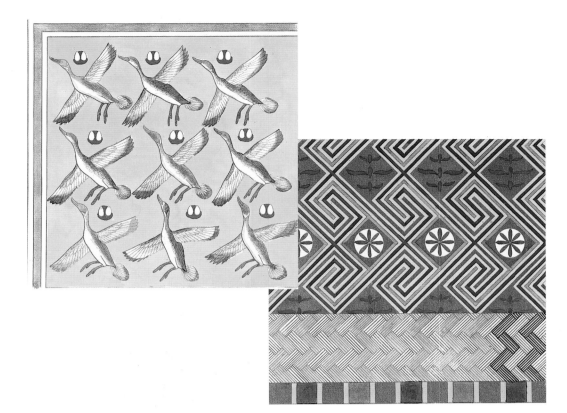

3.

10.

21.

22.

24.

92-93
EXAMPLES OF DECORATIVE ART
THEBAN TOMBS
VOLUME II, PLATE LXXIII

Further examples of ancient
Egyptian decorative art: in the
upper register, checkered, floral,
or geometric decorative motifs
in aristocratic homes; below,
three flower-shaped and plant-shaped
wall socles.

92 BOTTOM AND 93 BOTTOM AND RIGHT
FURNITURE AND ORNAMENTS
THEBAN TOMBS
VOLUME II, PLATE LXXIV

Besides some ornamental motifs
similar to those described in the
preceding plate, here is an interesting
range of furniture, including a wooden
folding chair whose legs end in
duck heads, and a bed or divan with
a lion's head and paws.

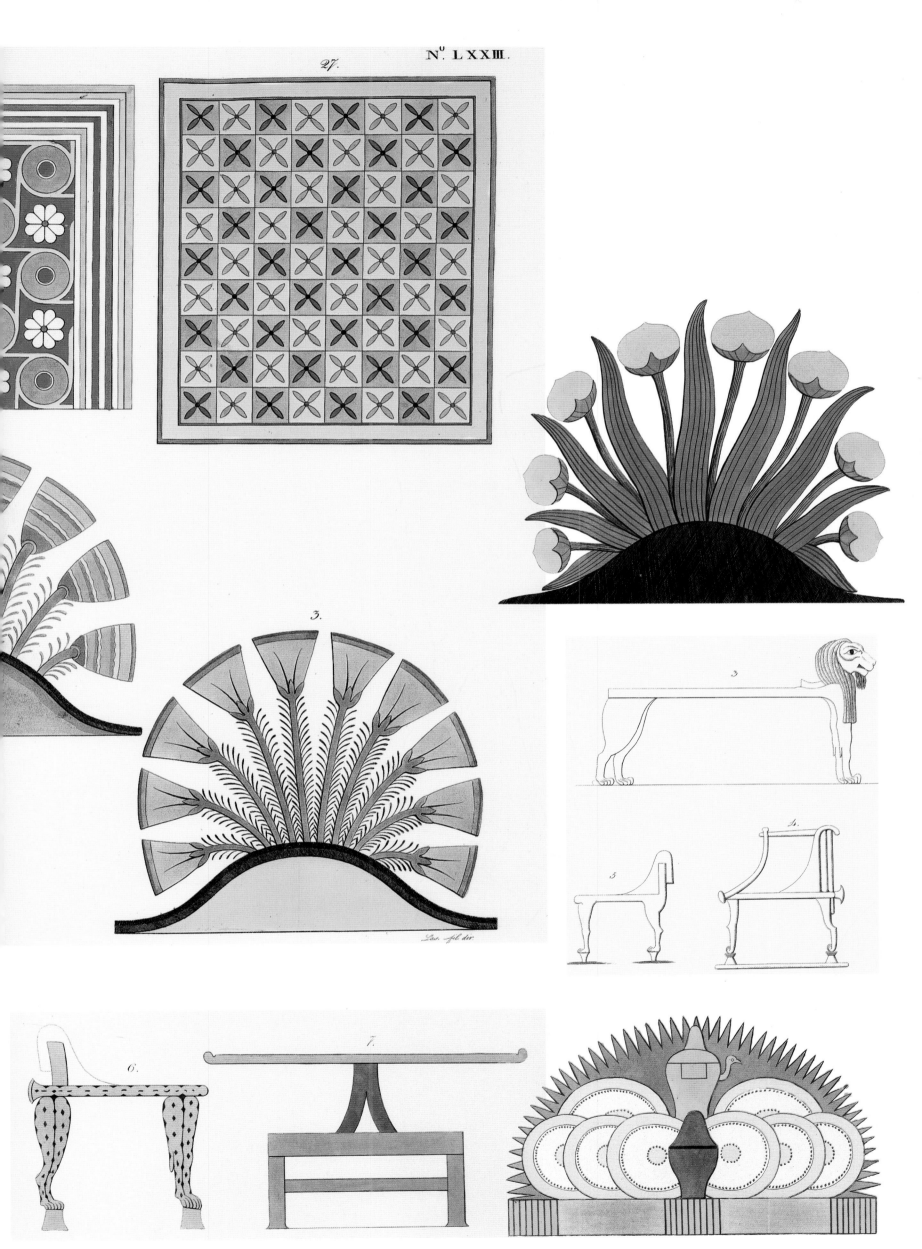

94-95
FURNITURE AND ORNAMENTS
THEBAN TOMBS
VOLUME II, PLATE LXXV

This plate shows furnishings used in
religious and royal circles.
At top left, a royal bed with four
incense burners, the figure of the
pharaoh making offerings, and two
figures of the goddess Merhyt; on the
pedestal is a series of cartouches with
the names and prenomen of Ramesses
IX. These are followed by a sedan chair
with a statuette of the pharaoh, the
goddess Isis who is protecting him
with her wings, and the goddess
Nekhbet in the guise of a vulture.
The upper register ends with a tiger
pelt used as a rug. Below left are a
cedar wood naos or shrine, a granite
sphinx, and two cubic thrones.

M. C.

1

3

Ra.

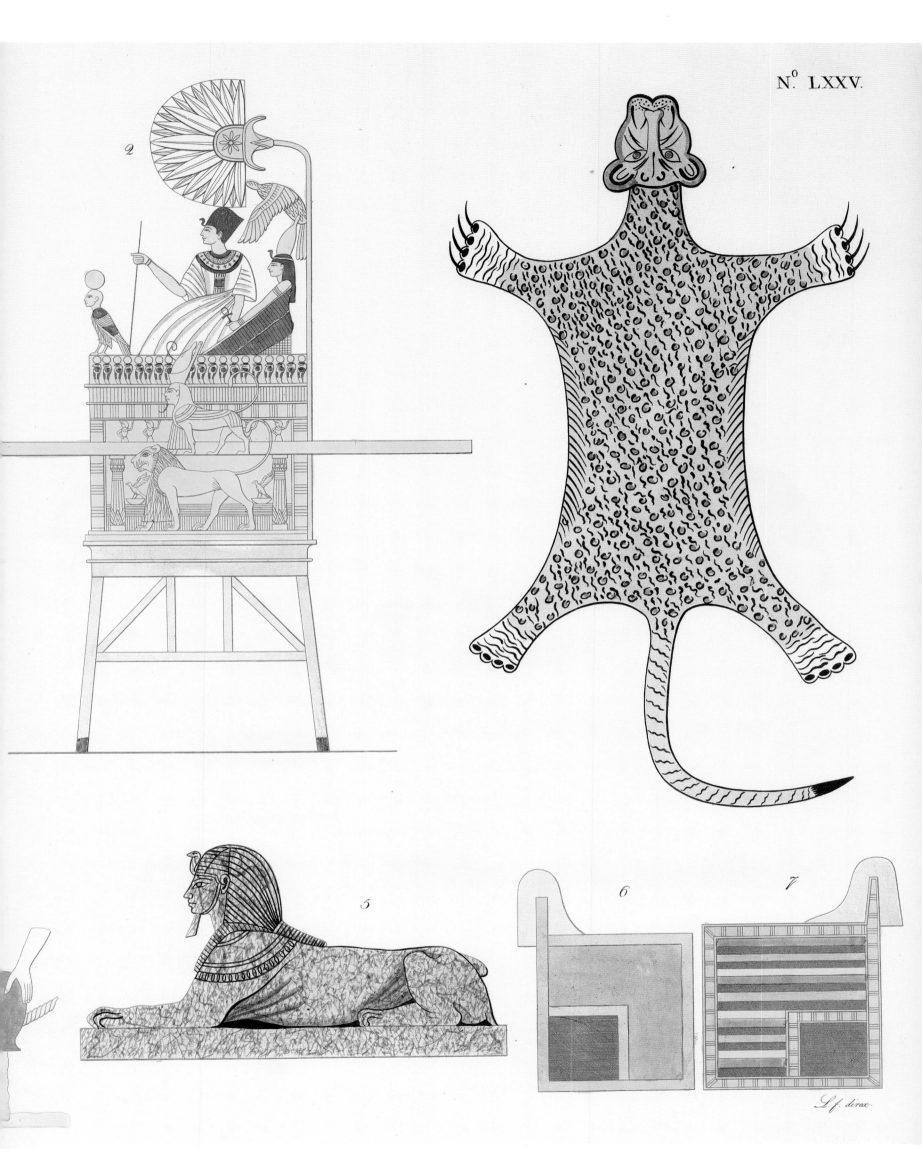

FUNERARY OFFERINGS
TOMBS IN AL-KAB AND THEBES
VOLUME II, PLATE LXXVIII

Above, a servant is offering his lord a bowl and is putting a bar of perfumed fat on his head. Below, in front of a richly laid table of offerings, the deceased couple receive sistra and necklaces from their daughters.

JEWELS AND FLABELLA
THEBAN TOMBS
VOLUME II, PLATE LXXX

These are illustrations of pectorals, necklaces, and bracelets, generally made of gold and embellished with semiprecious stones or enamel. These are followed by a series of flabella–large fans that were usually made in the shape of a papyrus and with ostrich feathers. In almost all cultures jewels have always had a particular fascination. The ancient Egyptians also attached great importance to various kinds of jewelry, which they usually wore both as ornaments and for their powers to ward off evil: the luxurious funerary equipment in the tombs of some pharaohs are examples of this latter function.

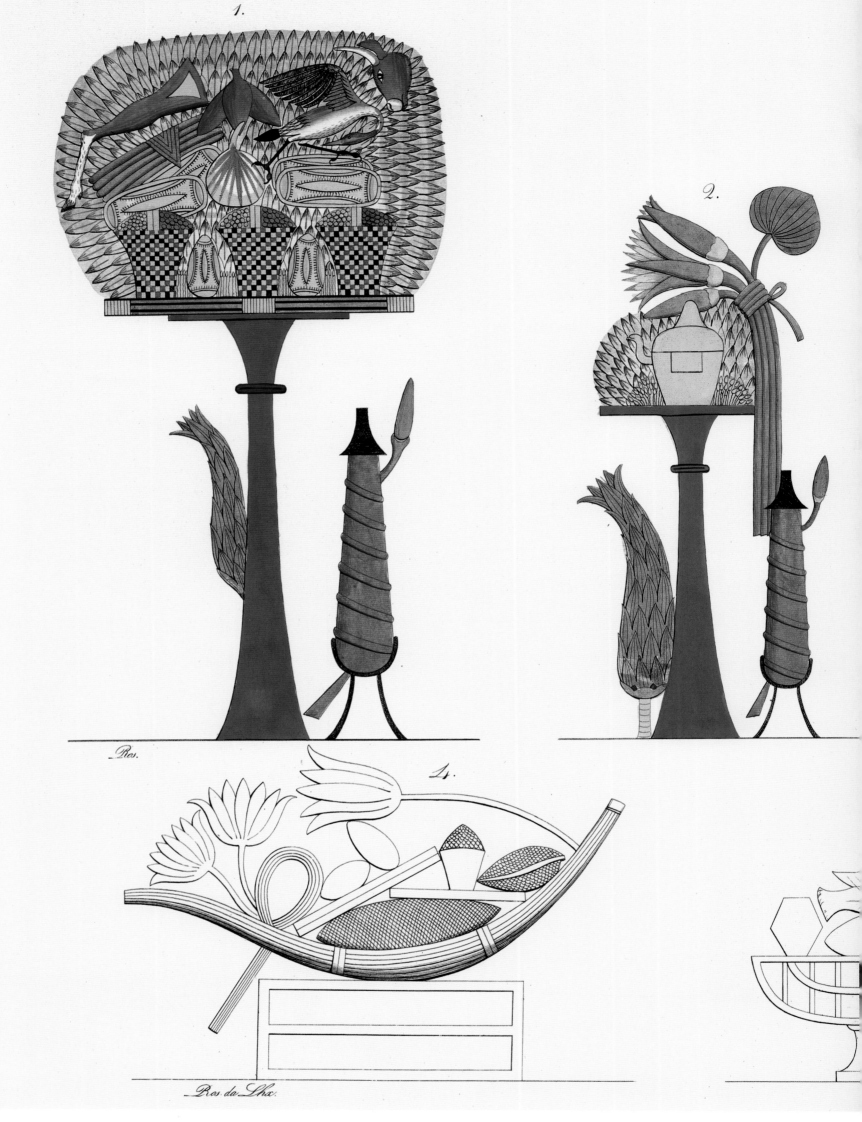

1.

2.

Ros.

4.

Ros. da Lhx.

98-99
FOOD OFFERINGS
THEBES, VALLEY OF THE KINGS
VOLUME II. PLATE LXXXVIII

The funerary equipment the ancient Egyptians placed inside the tombs also included food and drink, which were needed to guarantee the survival of the deceased in the afterlife. According to their religious beliefs, mural paintings of food offerings would assure—magically and eternally—the continuation of earthly existence. Among the drawings copied from royal tombs, are these two tables of offerings from a tomb at Biban al-Muluk: in the first (figure 1), among

vegetable leaves, are baskets
filled with fruit, some bread or sweets,
an ox's leg and head, and a duck.
The second table (figure 2) has
a jug and lotus buds.

Both tables have slender amphorae
beside them made more lovely by a
charming lotus bud that
is still closed. The next scene is
quite different in that it is not a

still-life: while one man is making
an offering of parts of an ox,
another is fanning the flames of two
perfume burners which are probably
consecrated to the deceased.

100 LEFT
DIFFERENT KINDS OF BEDS
THEBES, TOMB OF RAMESSES III
VOLUME II, PLATE XCII

This plate presents drawings of wooden beds (figures 4, 5, 6, and 7), for both domestic and funerary use whose legs rest on lions' paws. The funerary beds (figures 1, 2, and 3) are more richly decorated and elegant, and call to mind the cow-headed goddess Mehet-Weret, the hippopotamus-headed goddess Taweret, and the goddess Isis-Mehet in the guise of a lioness. The first two beds have mirrors with handles in the shape of a papyrus and lotus flower next to them.

100-101 TOP AND 101 CENTER
FURNITURE
THEBAN TOMBS
VOLUME II, PLATE XC

Examples of chairs and thrones are illustrated here. The chair with a low back (figure 1) and the round offering table (figure 7) date from the Old and Middle Kingdom respectively. The chairs with tall backs and lion's feet and the folding stool (figures 2, 3, and 4) mostly date from the New Kingdom. The plate also depicts a cube-shaped throne decorated with different geometric motifs.

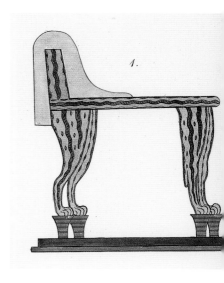

100-101 BOTTOM
ROYAL THRONES
THEBES, TOMB OF RAMESSES III
VOLUME II, PLATE XCI

These thrones have the same shape as the table in the preceding plate, and their elegance is heightened by the precious cloth upholstery. The side panels are covered with symbolic decoration in gold, semiprecious stones, or ivory.

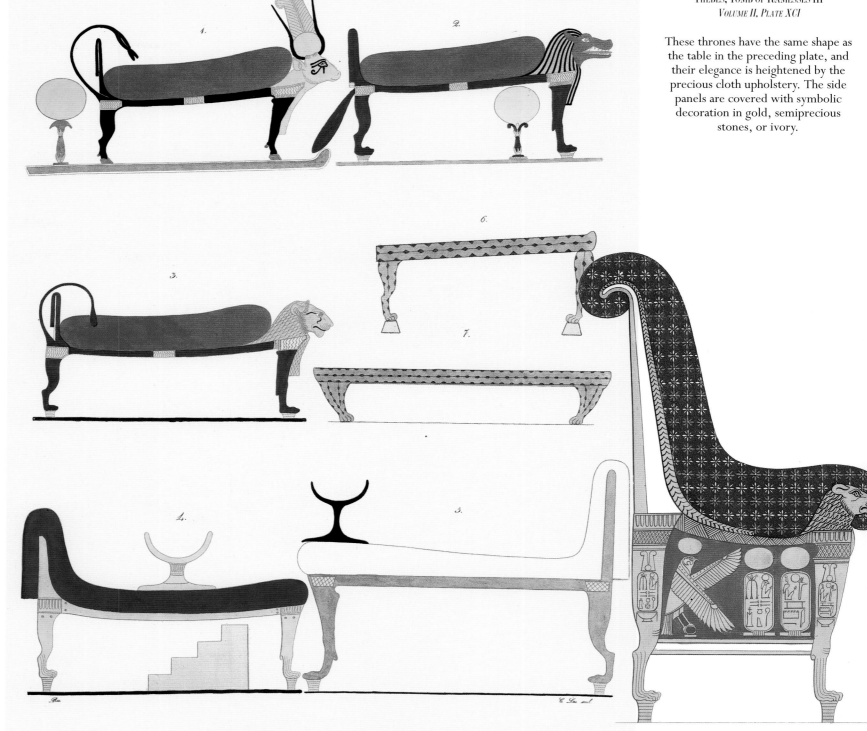

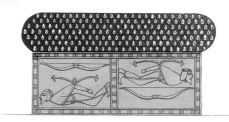

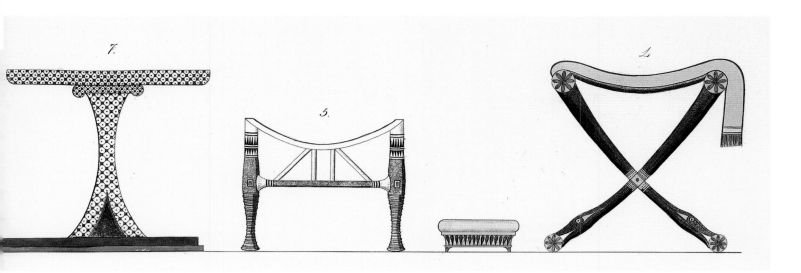

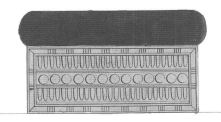

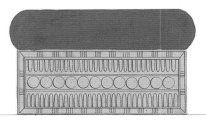

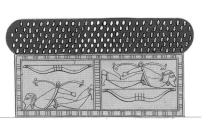

102-103
HARPISTS
THEBES, TOMB OF RAMESSES III
VOLUME III, PLATE XCVII

These are the famous images of two
blind harpists, who were perhaps
priests. With shaven heads and long
pleated gowns, they are holding two
large, beautifully colored harps whose
sound boxes are decorated with the
image of the pharaoh; he is shown
wearing the red crown of Lower Egypt
(left) and the double crown, the symbol
of Upper and Lower Egypt (right).
The tomb of Ramesses III was
discovered in 1768 by the Scottish
explorer James Bruce and the Italian
Luigi Balugani during their adventurous
and dramatic journey to present-day
Ethiopia in search of the source
of the Nile.

104 AND 105
WOMEN MUSICIANS AND DANCERS
THEBAN TOMBS
VOLUME III, PLATE XCVIII

A group of women with shaven heads
are playing and dancing to the rhythm of
a lute and quadrangular drum (top left).
Below are women playing stringed and
wind instruments. Note the harps,
which have different shapes and from
three to thirteen strings. Music and
dance were widespread art forms
in ancient Egypt.

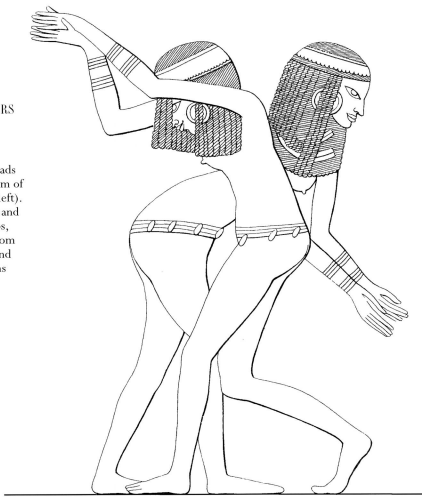

106-107
WOMEN MUSICIANS AND DANCERS
THEBES, TOMB OF NEBAMUN, AND BENI HASAN
VOLUME III, PLATE XCIX

This beautiful drawing shows the famous fragment of wall painting which, during Rosellini's time, was in the tomb of Nebamun, and is now kept in the British Museum, London. The extremely rare frontal rendering of the musicians shows that the artist was trying to surpass the limits of conventional ancient Egyptian iconography, which called for portraits only in profile. While the woman at right is playing the double flute, the others—splendidly dressed and with the characteristic perfumed cone on their heads—accompany her by clapping their hands and perhaps singing.

106 TOP AND 107 TOP
MUSICIANS AND DANCERS
THEBES, TOMB OF NEBAMUN, AND BENI HASAN
VOLUME III, PLATE XCIX

In the upper pictures, women rehearse dance steps while others move to the rhythm of drums.

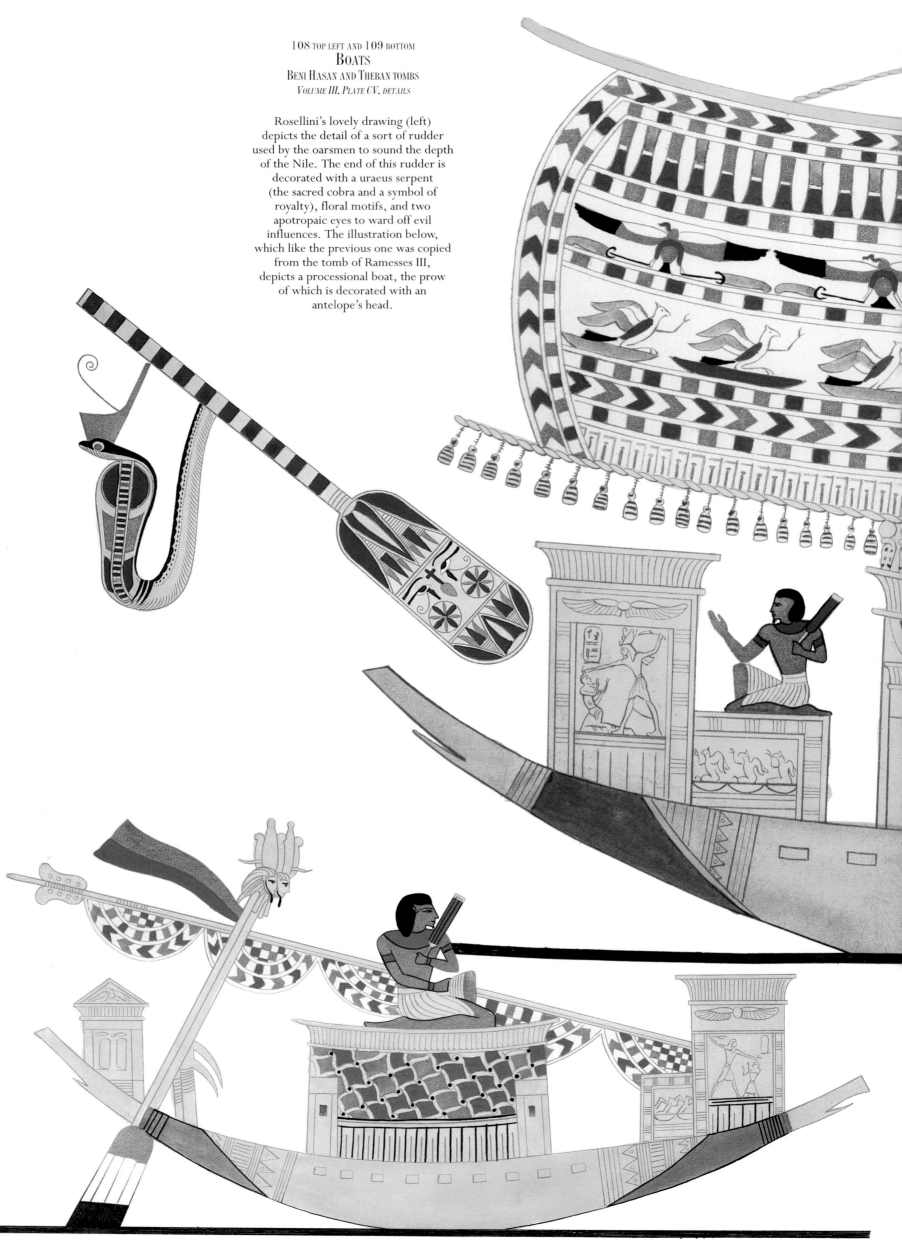

Rosellini's lovely drawing (left) depicts the detail of a sort of rudder used by the oarsmen to sound the depth of the Nile. The end of this rudder is decorated with a uraeus serpent (the sacred cobra and a symbol of royalty), floral motifs, and two apotropaic eyes to ward off evil influences. The illustration below, which like the previous one was copied from the tomb of Ramesses III, depicts a processional boat, the prow of which is decorated with an antelope's head.

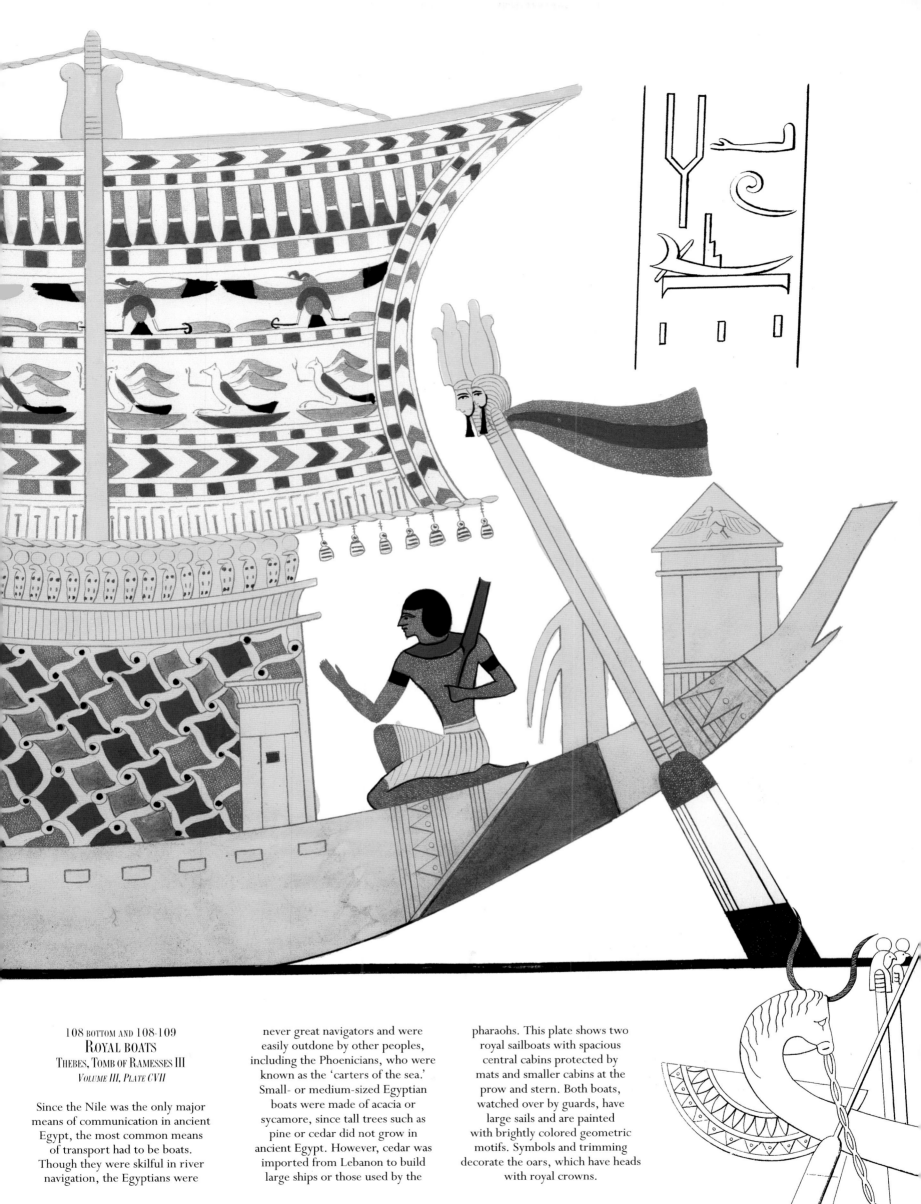

108 bottom and 108-109
ROYAL BOATS
THEBES, TOMB OF RAMESSES III
VOLUME III, PLATE CVII

Since the Nile was the only major
means of communication in ancient
Egypt, the most common means
of transport had to be boats.
Though they were skilful in river
navigation, the Egyptians were
never great navigators and were
easily outdone by other peoples,
including the Phoenicians, who were
known as the 'carters of the sea.'
Small- or medium-sized Egyptian
boats were made of acacia or
sycamore, since tall trees such as
pine or cedar did not grow in
ancient Egypt. However, cedar was
imported from Lebanon to build
large ships or those used by the
pharaohs. This plate shows two
royal sailboats with spacious
central cabins protected by
mats and smaller cabins at the
prow and stern. Both boats,
watched over by guards, have
large sails and are painted
with brightly colored geometric
motifs. Symbols and trimming
decorate the oars, which have heads
with royal crowns.

110-111
ROYAL BOATS
THEBES, TOMB OF RAMESSES III
PLATE CVIII

In the illustration at left,
"two boats, driven by the wind"
(Rosellini, III, 146) and with their sails
unfurled, "proceed in convoy"
(Champollion, III, 3); in the
illustration at right, the boat, complete
with a royal throne and royal symbols,
sails down the river. In the latter,
there is a seated guard holding
a *herep* scepter, the "insignia of
that office."

112-113 TOP AND CENTER
FUNERARY SCENES
TOMBS IN THEBES AND AL-KAB
VOLUME III, PLATE CXXVII

The upper representation, copied from the tomb of Amenemope, depicts the mummy which, after the propitiatory rituals carried out by one of the deceased's two sons, is about to be placed in a naos, then put on a boat pulled by cows. A woman, perhaps his wife, is weeping. In the other two figures, copied from tombs at al-Kab, the mummy is being transported toward its burial site.

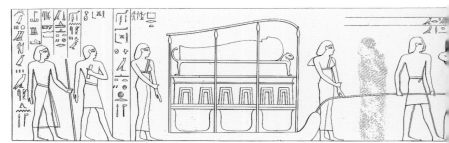

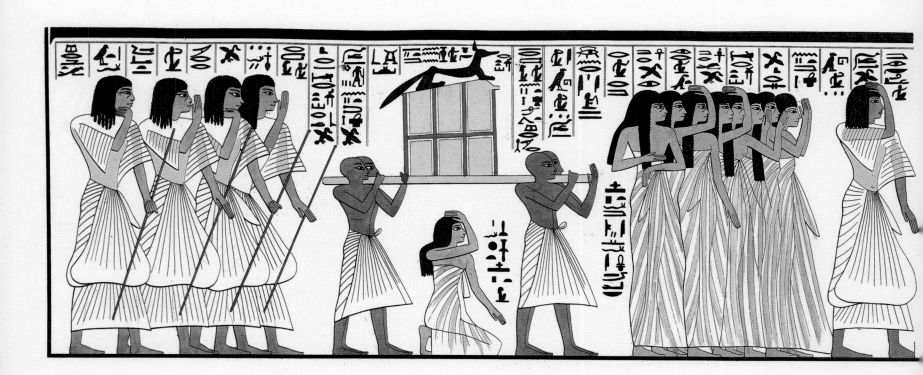

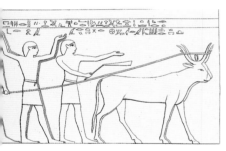

112 bottom and 113 bottom
FUNERARY SCENES
THEBAN TOMB
Volume III, Plate CXXVIII

The scene at right shows a mummy being transported. Placed first in a naos on a boat, it is then gently put on a sled pulled by four heifers. A priest, wearing the typical panther pelt, offers incense and carries out purification rituals. At left, among the grieving persons and the group of professional mourners, four men are bearing the chest, surmounted by the figure of Anubis in the guise of a jackal, that held the canopic jars containing the deceased's viscera.

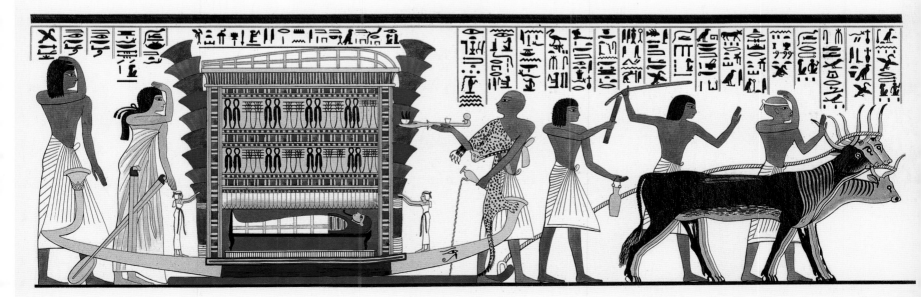

114-115
FUNERARY SCENES
THEBAN TOMB
VOLUME III, PLATE CXXIX

This plate depicts the conclusion
of the funeral ceremony. Besides
the mourning scene (above), there
is the priest carrying out the 'opening
of the mouth' funerary ritual,
which guaranteed the continuation
of life in the hereafter. Anubis, the
jackal-headed god of mummification,
sees to the final details of embalming
the deceased, who is on a sort
of catafalque, under which the
four canopic jars containing the
deceased's viscera can be seen.
The goddesses Isis (left) and Nephthys
(right) watch over the ceremony.

116 TOP
FUNERARY BOATS
BENI HASAN
VOLUME III. PLATE CXXX

This plate depicts two boats used
for the burial ritual. Both have
a chamber adorned with latticework
matting. Above, men and women mourn.

116 CENTER AND BOTTOM
FUNERARY BOATS
BENI HASAN
VOLUME III. PLATE CXXXI

More illustrations of boats used in
the burial ritual. The two upper scenes
depict the transport of funerary goods,
while below women grieve before
the mummy of the deceased.

117
FUNERARY SCENES
THEBAN TOMBS
VOLUME III. PLATE CXXXIV

The goddess of the sycamore tree
(top and right) offers fruit to the dead
couple. The scene below, similar to
the one already described in plate
CXXIX, shows the god Anubis next
to the deceased. The latter's *ba*, or soul,
depicted as a human-headed bird,
flies over the deceased and places
near his nose a sailboat and a
scepter—symbols of the vital breath
indispensable to guarantee rebirth.

Religious Monuments

118
SETI I AMONG GODS
THEBES, TOMB OF SETI I
PLATE LIX

In this scene the pharaoh is presented
by the god Horus to Osiris, the
principal god in the domain of the dead,
who is here seated on the throne
in mummy wrapping. Behind Osiris
is Amentet, the goddess of the West,
who is ready to receive the dead. This
beautiful drawing by Nestor L'Hôte
is completed by multicolored friezes
and inscriptions, among which are the
pharaoh's names in the two cartouches.

119
SETI I AND HATHOR
THEBES, TOMB OF SETI I
PLATE LVIII

This plate illustrates a relief that
is now kept in the National
Archaeological Museum in Florence
but which at the time of the Franco-
Tuscan expedition was in Seti I's
burial chamber. The pharaoh,
in a rich transparent robe, is received
by the goddess Hathor, who offers
him her necklace, which will guarantee
him protection and prosperity.
The tomb, discovered by Belzoni,
is considered the most beautiful in
the Valley of the Kings.

The scene, enclosed among the signs
of the firmament and mountain
(the latter is a symbol of the western
necropolis), is a double portrait of
Ramesses X, the penultimate Twentieth

Dynasty pharaoh, who is kneeling while offering the eye of Horus to the sun-god Ra. The latter is represented as a disk containing the beetle Khepri, a form of Ra as the rising sun, and the ram-headed god Atum as the setting sun. The scene is completed with the goddesses Isis (left) and Nephthys (right).

OSIRIS'S JUDGMENT
THEBES, TOMB OF RAMESSES VI
PLATE LXVI

This vast scene is a variation
of the 'weighing of the heart.'
Osiris is seated on his throne, holding
his scepter and the symbol of life,
and is about to receive nine persons
(the souls of nine dead people) whom
he is going to judge. A balance,
carried by a mummiform spirit,
is ready to weigh these individuals'
deeds on Earth.
The souls that are judged to be
guilty return in animal guise,
that is to say, they are sent back
to Earth in the form of animals,
which were considered symbols
of various sins. According to
Champollion, the image of the sow,
which is on a boat between two baboons,
represents the sin of greediness.
The jackal-headed god Anubis
and four mortuary genii with
gazelle heads, are witnessing
the judgment of the dead.

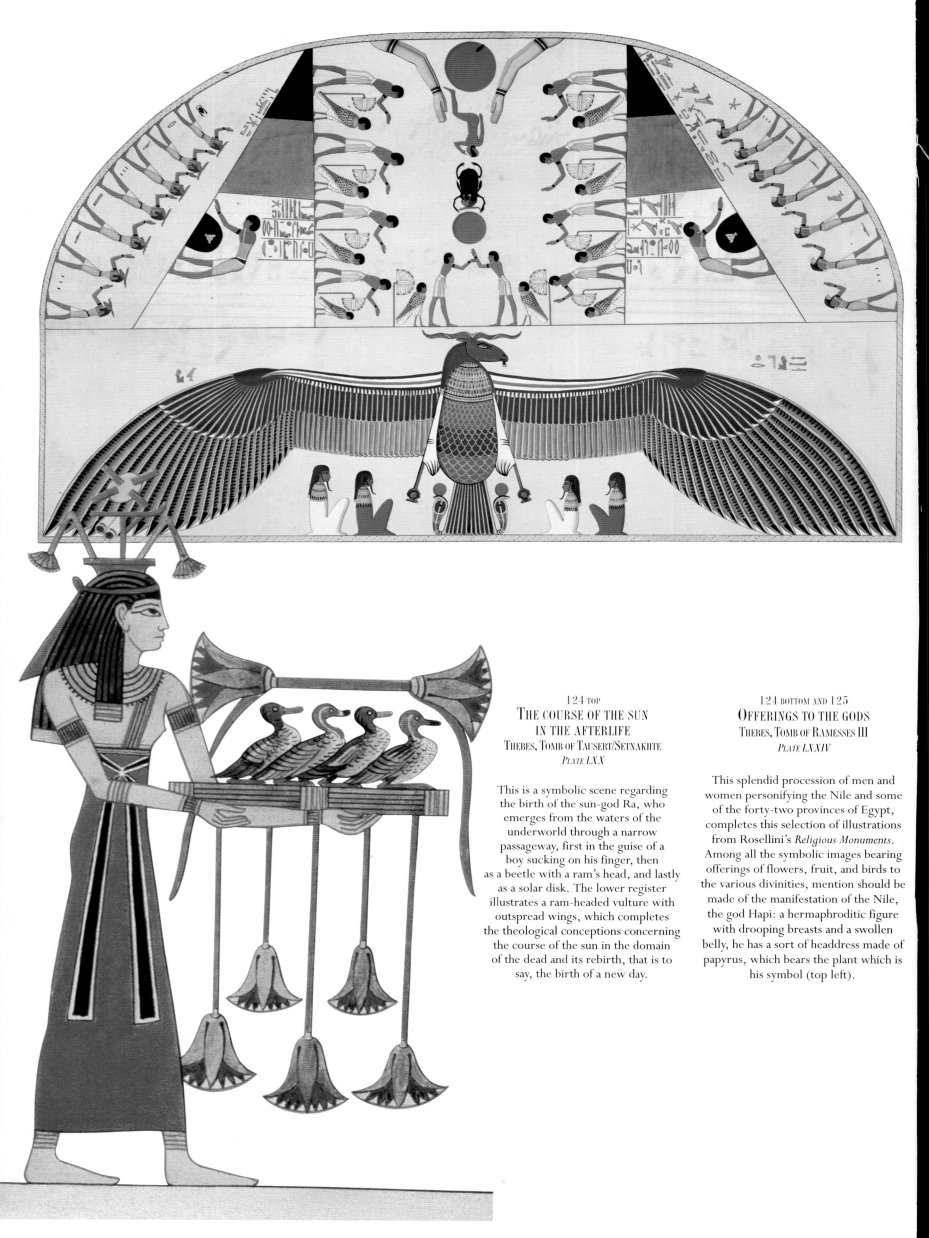

124 TOP
THE COURSE OF THE SUN IN THE AFTERLIFE
THEBES, TOMB OF TAUSERT/SETNAKHTE
PLATE LXX

This is a symbolic scene regarding the birth of the sun-god Ra, who emerges from the waters of the underworld through a narrow passageway, first in the guise of a boy sucking on his finger, then as a beetle with a ram's head, and lastly as a solar disk. The lower register illustrates a ram-headed vulture with outspread wings, which completes the theological conceptions concerning the course of the sun in the domain of the dead and its rebirth, that is to say, the birth of a new day.

124 BOTTOM AND 125
OFFERINGS TO THE GODS
THEBES, TOMB OF RAMESSES III
PLATE LXXIV

This splendid procession of men and women personifying the Nile and some of the forty-two provinces of Egypt, completes this selection of illustrations from Rosellini's *Religious Monuments*. Among all the symbolic images bearing offerings of flowers, fruit, and birds to the various divinities, mention should be made of the manifestation of the Nile, the god Hapi: a hermaphroditic figure with drooping breasts and a swollen belly, he has a sort of headdress made of papyrus, which bears the plant which is his symbol (top left).

List of Plates

RELIGIOUS MONUMENTS

PHOTO CREDITS

All photographs are by Archivio
White Star except the following:
Page 8 Alberto Siliotti/Geodia
Page 10 Alberto Siliotti/Geodia
Page 11 top left Alberto Siliotti/
Geodia
Page 11 top right Alberto Siliotti/
Geodia
Page 11 bottom left Alberto Siliotti/
Geodia
Page 11 bottom right Alberto Siliotti/
Geodia
Page 12-13 Scala Group
Page 13 top left Alberto Siliotti/
Geodia
Page 13 top right Alberto Siliotti/
Geodia

OFFERINGS TO THE GODS
AND REPRESENTATIONS OF THE NILE
THEBES, TOMB OF RAMESSES III
RELIGIOUS MONUMENTS,
PLATE LXXIV, DETAIL

The very existence of ancient
Egypt depended on the Nile,
to which a hymn was dedicated:
"Greetings to thee, O Nile, you who
have emerged from the Earth,
who have come to give life
to Egypt! [...] It is he who irrigates
the fields to give life to all the livestock,
who quenches the desert's thirst [...]
It is he who produces barley and makes
wheat grow [...] If he is lazy [...]
everyone becomes poor [...] and millions
of men perish [...] When he begins
to rise [...] everyone rejoices."